THE CAMBRIDGE BIBLE COMMENTARY

NEW ENGLISH BIBLE

GENERAL EDITORS

P. R. ACKROYD, A. R. C. LEANEY
J. W. PACKER

PSALMS 101–150

PSALMS 101–150

COMMENTARY BY

J. W. ROGERSON

Senior Lecturer in Theology, University of Durham

AND

J. W. McKAY

Lecturer in Theology, University of Hull

CAMBRIDGE UNIVERSITY PRESS

CAMBRIDGE

LONDON · NEW YORK · MELBOURNE

Published by the Syndics of the Cambridge University Press
The Pitt Building, Trumpington Street, Cambridge CB2 IRP
Bentley House, 200 Euston Road, London NW1 2DB
32 East 57th Street, New York, NY 10022, USA
296 Beaconsfield Parade, Middle Park, Melbourne 3206, Australia

© Cambridge University Press 1977

First published 1977

Printed in Great Britain
at the University Press, Cambridge

Library of Congress cataloguing in publication data
Bible. O.T. Psalms. English. New English. 1977. Psalms.
(The Cambridge Bible commentary, New English Bible)
Includes bibliographies and indexes.
CONTENTS: [1] 1–50. – [2] 51–100. – [3] 101–150.
I. Bible. O.T. Psalms – Commentaries. I. Rogerson, John William.
II. McKay, John William. II. Title. III. Series.
BS1430.3.R63   223′.2′077   76–27911
ISBN 0 521 21465 3 hard covers (Psalms 101–150)
ISBN 0 521 29162 3 paperback (Psalms 101–150)

GENERAL EDITORS' PREFACE

The aim of this series is to provide the text of the New English Bible closely linked to a commentary in which the results of modern scholarship are made available to the general reader. Teachers and young people have been especially kept in mind. The commentators have been asked to assume no specialized theological knowledge, and no knowledge of Greek and Hebrew. Bare references to other literature and multiple references to other parts of the Bible have been avoided. Actual quotations have been given as often as possible.

The completion of the New Testament part of the series in 1967 provides a basis upon which the production of the much larger Old Testament and Apocrypha series can be undertaken. The welcome accorded to the series has been an encouragement to the editors to follow the same general pattern, and an attempt has been made to take account of criticisms which have been offered. One necessary change is the inclusion of the translators' footnotes since in the Old Testament these are more extensive, and essential for the understanding of the text.

Within the severe limits imposed by the size and scope of the series, each commentator will attempt to set out the main findings of recent biblical scholarship and to describe the historical background to the text. The main theological issues will also be critically discussed.

Much attention has been given to the form of the volumes. The aim is to produce books each of which will be read consecutively from first to last page. The introductory material leads naturally into the text, which itself leads into the alternating sections of the commentary.

The series is accompanied by three volumes of a more general character. *Understanding the Old Testament* sets out to provide the larger historical and archaeological background, to say something about the life and thought of the people of the Old Testament, and to answer the question 'Why should we study the Old Testament?'. *The Making of the Old Testament* is concerned with the formation of the books of the Old Testament and Apocrypha in the context of the ancient Near Eastern world, and with the ways in which these books have come down to us in the life of the Jewish and Christian communities. *Old Testament Illustrations* contains maps, diagrams and photographs with an explanatory text. These three volumes are designed to provide material helpful to the understanding of the individual books and their commentaries, but they are also prepared so as to be of use quite independently.

P. R. A.
A. R. C. L.
J. W. P.

CONTENTS

CONTENTS

CONTENTS

✧   ✧   ✧   ✧   ✧   ✧   ✧   ✧   ✧   ✧   ✧   ✧   ✧

THE FOOTNOTES TO THE
N.E.B. TEXT

The footnotes to the N.E.B. text are designed to help the reader either to understand particular points of detail – the meaning of a name, the presence of a play upon words – or to give information about the actual text. Where the Hebrew text appears to be erroneous, or there is doubt about its precise meaning, it may be necessary to turn to manuscripts which offer a different wording, or to ancient translations of the text which may suggest a better reading, or to offer a new explanation based upon conjecture. In such cases, the footnotes supply very briefly an indication of the evidence, and whether the solution proposed is one that is regarded as possible or as probable. Various abbreviations are used in the footnotes:

(1) Some abbreviations are simply of terms used in explaining a point: *ch(s).*, chapter(s); *cp.*, compare; *lit.*, literally; *mng.*, meaning; *MS(S).*, manuscript(s), i.e. Hebrew manuscript(s), unless otherwise stated; *om.*, omit(s); *or*, indicating an alternative interpretation; *poss.*, possible; *prob.*, probable; *rdg.*, reading; *Vs(s).*, version(s).

(2) Other abbreviations indicate sources of information from which better interpretations or readings may be obtained.

Aq.   Aquila, a Greek translator of the Old Testament (perhaps about A.D. 130) characterized by great literalness.

Aram.   Aramaic – may refer to the text in this language (used in parts of Ezra and Daniel), or to the meaning of an Aramaic word. Aramaic belongs to the same language family as Hebrew, and is known from about 1000 B.C. over a wide area of the Middle East, including Palestine.

Heb.   Hebrew – may refer to the Hebrew text or may indicate the literal meaning of the Hebrew word.

Josephus   Flavius Josephus (A.D. 37/8–about 100), author of the *Jewish Antiquities*, a survey of the whole history of his people, directed partly at least to a non-Jewish audience, and of various other works, notably one on the *Jewish War* (that of A.D. 66–73) and a defence of Judaism (*Against Apion*).

Luc. Sept.   Lucian's recension of the Septuagint, an important edition made in Antioch in Syria about the end of the third century A.D.

Pesh.   Peshitta or Peshitto, the Syriac version of the Old Testament. Syriac is the name given chiefly to a form of Eastern Aramaic used by the Christian community. The translation varies in quality, and is at many points influenced by the Septuagint or the Targums.

Sam.   Samaritan Pentateuch – the form of the first five books of the Old Testament as used by the Samaritan community. It is written in Hebrew in a special form of the Old Hebrew script, and preserves an important form of the text, somewhat influenced by Samaritan ideas.

Scroll(s)   Scroll(s), commonly called the Dead Sea Scrolls, found at or near Qumran from 1947 onwards. These important manuscripts shed light on the state of the Hebrew text as it was developing in the last centuries B.C. and the first century A.D.

Sept.   Septuagint (meaning 'seventy'; often abbreviated as the Roman numeral LXX), the name given to the main Greek version of the Old Testament. According to tradition, the Pentateuch was translated in Egypt in the third century B.C. by 70 (or 72) translators, six from each tribe, but the precise nature of its origin and development is not fully known. It was intended to provide Greek-speaking Jews with a convenient translation. Subsequently it came to be much revered by the Christian community.

Symm.   Symmachus, another Greek translator of the Old Testament (beginning of the third century A.D.), who tried to combine literalness with good style. Both Lucian and Jerome viewed his version with favour.

Targ.   Targum, a name given to various Aramaic versions of the Old Testament, produced over a long period and eventually standardized, for the use of Aramaic-speaking Jews.

Theod.   Theodotion, the author of a revision of the Septuagint (probably second century A.D.), very dependent on the Hebrew text.

Vulg.   Vulgate, the most important Latin version of the Old Testament, produced by Jerome about A.D. 400, and the text most used throughout the Middle Ages in western Christianity.

[. . .]   In the text itself square brackets are used to indicate probably late additions to the Hebrew text.

(Fuller discussion of a number of these points may be found in *The Making of the Old Testament* in this series.)

PSALMS

✳ ✳ ✳ ✳ ✳ ✳ ✳ ✳ ✳ ✳ ✳ ✳ ✳ ✳ ✳

NAME, CONTENT AND PLACE OF THE BOOK
IN THE OLD TESTAMENT

The name 'psalms' comes from the Greek Septuagint translation of the Bible via the Latin Vulgate (see *The Making of the Old Testament*, pp. 147–54). The Greek word *psalmos* denoted the twanging of a stringed instrument with the fingers, and later came to mean a song sung to the accompaniment of a plucked instrument. In turn, *psalmos* is a translation of the Hebrew *mizmōr*, which also appears to have denoted both the playing of instruments and the singing of songs. Strictly speaking, then, the title 'psalms' means 'songs'. The name for the book in the Hebrew Bible is *tehillīm* or *sēpher tehillīm*, meaning 'praises' or 'book of praises'.

In actual fact, neither 'songs' nor 'praises' adequately describes the content of the Psalter. In it, we find expressed by both the individual and the congregation, prayers for help and thanksgivings for deliverance in the face of sickness, despair, desertion by friends, and physical danger. We find hymns of praise to God as creator and judge of the world, as the one who has chosen his people Israel and his dwelling in Zion, and who has guided, supported and punished his people. We find entreaties that God will speedily and effectively establish his rule throughout the world, at the same time that it is acknowledged that he is already the universal king, controlling the forces of nature, and shaping the destinies of the nations. We find prayers for the well-being of the king, and traces of ceremonial used at the king's coronation and the periodic renewal of the divine covenant with the house of David. We find extended meditations on Israel's past history, and on God's gracious revelation of his law and his will to his people. We find the whole range of human emotions in their relation to God, from extreme pessimism and doubt to simple and certain trust. Even this lengthy catalogue is not complete, thus showing the impossibility of describing the Psalter and its contents in one word or short phrase. At the end of this introduction, an attempt is made to tabulate the contents of the Psalter.

The psalms stand either in first or second place in the third section of the Hebrew Bible, the Writings (see *The Making of the Old Testament*, pp. 118–24). The English Bible has a different order for the books, with Psalms following the Pentateuch and the historical books (including Ruth, Esther and Job). This arrangement derives from the way the books of the Old Testament were grouped together in the early Christian centuries. The underlying principle was probably that the psalms (believed to be substantially by David) should precede the books attributed to Solomon (Proverbs, Ecclesiastes, Song of Songs) which in turn should precede the prophetic books bearing the names of Isaiah, Jeremiah and Ezekiel. In other words, these books appear in the order of the historical sequence of the lives of those who were believed to have been their authors.

Although there are 150 psalms, there are two major ways of numbering them, the Hebrew and the Greek. The N.E.B. follows the Hebrew numbering, while among Bibles and commentaries used by Roman Catholics, the Greek numbering has been familiar. The major differences are that Pss. 11–113 and 117–146 in the Hebrew numbering are 10–112 and 116–145 in the Greek numbering, and these differences arose from uncertainty about how to regard the verses contained in Pss. 9, 10, 114, 115, 116 and 147 (according to the Hebrew reckoning). The Greek numbering was almost certainly correct in regarding Pss. 9–10 as one psalm (and note that the N.E.B. regards them as one psalm, numbered 9–10) but it was probably incorrect in regarding Pss. 114 and 115 as one psalm, and in dividing 116 and 147 each into two psalms. On the other hand, modern scholarship is virtually unanimous in regarding Pss. 42 and 43 as originally one psalm, against both the Hebrew and the Greek numberings.

PSALM TITLES, AUTHORSHIP AND GROWTH OF THE PSALTER

The preface to the Library Edition of the N.E.B. Old Testament (p. xiv) notes that in the Hebrew, many psalms have titles or headings. The N.E.B. translators decided not to include them in the translation because (i) they are almost certainly not the work of the authors of the psalms, (ii) where they are historical notices they are deduced from the text of the psalm itself and rest on no reliable tradition, and (iii) where they are musical directions, they are mostly unintelligible. However, it is to be noted that the N.E.B. retained the 'doxologies' at the end of Pss. 41, 72, 89 and 106 which mark the conclusion of Books 1–4 of the Psalms respectively, as well as the notice 'Here end the prayers of David son of Jesse' at 72: 20. It can be said of all these that they are no more the work of the authors of the individual psalms than are the psalm titles. Like the titles, they were added at various times as the psalms were collected together to form the Psalter as we have it, and it is odd that in the N.E.B. they were retained where the titles were omitted.

Although the N.E.B. translators are correct in saying that the musical parts of the psalm titles are today unintelligible and that the historical notices are no more than guesses, the titles have something to contribute when we try to deduce how the psalms were collected together. The following psalms are associated with David through the phrase *le dāwīd* in the titles: 3–41 (except 33, and 10 which is a continuation of 9; see above), 51–65, 68–70, 86, 101, 103, 108–110, 122, 124, 131, 133, 138–145. Pss. 42–49, 84–85 and 87–88 are associated with the sons of Korah, while 50 and 73–83 are associated

3

with Asaph. These account for almost all of the 'named' psalms; there are thirty-four nameless or 'orphan' psalms. It will be observed that the 'Davidic' psalms fall predominantly in the first half of the Psalter (fifty-five of Pss. 1–72 are 'Davidic') while the 'orphan' psalms are found mainly in the second half. This may indicate that in the first instance, collections of 'Davidic' psalms were made, and that in the later stages of the compilation of the Psalter, anonymous psalms were added.

The meaning of the Hebrew phrase *le dāwīd* has been much discussed. Traditionally, it was taken to denote Davidic authorship. In modern scholarship, it has often been taken to mean 'belonging to the Davidic collection', while a third view is that the phrase was meant by those who added it, to denote authorship, but that these editors were not guided by any reliable tradition. There is probably some truth in all three of these views.

The Old Testament contains several references to David's skill as a musician and singer (e.g. 1 Sam. 16: 17–23; 2 Sam. 1: 17–27; Amos 6: 5) and it is reasonable to assume that David was the author of some of the psalms, even if we have no means of discovering exactly which. It is also possible that from early times these psalms were headed *le dāwīd*. Later scribes are also likely to have claimed Davidic authorship for psalms by prefacing them with this title, although reliable tradition was lacking. That the phrase *le dāwīd* might also indicate a collection can be argued as follows. Beginning with Ps. 42, we have the Elohistic Psalter (Pss. 42–83), so called because an editor or editors seem to have altered the divine name in the psalms from an original 'the LORD' to 'God' (Hebrew *'elōhīm*, thus the term 'Elohistic'). This can be seen if Ps. 14 is compared with Ps. 53 in the English; and the editing is crudely apparent in the Hebrew of Ps. 80, though not in the English translation. This editorial treatment of the divine name begins immediately after the first block of 'Davidic' psalms (3–41), and it is thus reasonable to assume that

4

Pss. 3–41 once existed as a separate collection from 42 to 83, because they escaped this editorial work. Further, since all but one of Pss. 3–41 are entitled *le dāwīd*, it is reasonable to say that the title indicates a collection as well as authorship. If we examine the psalms ascribed to the sons of Korah, we see that most of them have an interest in Zion, the temple and worship, from which it is usually concluded that the sons of Korah were a band of temple singers. For the name Asaph, see 1 Chron. 16: 4–7; 2 Chron. 35: 15.

With the help of these points, the following suggestions can be made about the growth of the Psalter. (i) There first existed several separate collections of psalms: two Davidic collections (Pss. 3–41 and 51–72 – cp. 72: 20) probably containing genuine psalms of David and others attributed to him; a Korahite collection (Pss. 42–49, 84–85, 87–88) and an Asaphite collection (Pss. 50, 73–83). (ii) An Elohistic Psalter was compiled from three collections – the second Davidic, part of the Korahite, and the Asaphite, to form the group of psalms, 42–83. This collection was subjected to editorial revision in which the divine name 'the LORD' was changed to 'God' ('*elōhīm*). It is also possible that the Elohistic Psalter extended as far as Ps. 88, and that the editorial alteration of the divine name proceeded no further than Ps. 83. (iii) The first Davidic collection and the Elohistic Psalter were joined together. (iv) Numerous further additions were made, about which we can only guess. It is probable that Ps. 1 was composed to be the beginning of the whole Psalter, and possible that Ps. 119 at one point marked its conclusion. If this is so, then Pss. 120–134 which are each entitled 'A song of ascents' would have been attached as a block following on from Ps. 119, and Pss. 138–145 may have been a small group of Davidic psalms which were added at a late stage to the Psalter. (Pss. 135–137 lack titles, and it is impossible to say why or when they were placed after Pss. 120–134.)

The division of the Psalter into five books (Pss. 1–41, 42–72, 73–89, 90–106, 107–150) presumably dates from the time of the completion of the Psalter, probably in the third century B.C. It is usually held that the Psalter was divided into five books on analogy with the five books of the Pentateuch. However, we have already suggested that long before the Psalter was complete, Pss. 3–41 and 42–83 probably existed as separate collections, and in the commentary on Ps. 72, it is suggested that the doxology of 72: 18f. was added to that psalm before the Psalter was divided into books by means of doxologies. Ps. 72: 18f. may have served as the model for the other doxologies.

Although we know so little about how the psalms came to be arranged in their present order, the process may not have been entirely haphazard. Pss. 105 and 106 are clearly complementary, and the unrelieved pessimism of Ps. 88 is immediately followed by the affirmation 'I will sing the story of thy love, O LORD' in 89: 1.

HISTORY OF INTERPRETATION

It has long been recognized that the psalms are rich and varied in content, including praise, prayer and lament. Commentators in all ages have recognized their applicability to many situations in the religious life of the individual and the community, and it is probable that even in the Old Testament period, psalms were reinterpreted in the light of new situations. Thus, Ps. 79, which speaks of enemies defiling Jerusalem and its temple, is never quite explicit enough to enable us to identify the events for certain, and the reason may be that reinterpretation and spiritualizing of the psalm have obscured its references to the events which first called it forth. In 1 Chron. 16: 8–36, parts of Pss. 96, 105, 106 and 107 are quoted in respect of the institution of praise to God by David, after he had brought the Ark to Jerusalem.

Alongside, and not necessarily instead of, what we might call the spiritual interpretation of the psalms, there has been the historical interpretation. Traditional Jewish interpretation understood many of the psalms in the context of the life of David, and this approach was expressed already in some of the psalm titles. Thus the title of Ps. 51 reads 'To the choirmaster. A Psalm of David, when Nathan the prophet came to him after he had gone in to Bathsheba', linking the psalm with the incidents related in 2 Sam. 11–12. When, in the eighteenth and nineteenth centuries, critical scholarship began to abandon belief in the Davidic authorship of the psalms, the historical approach continued, but now, many psalms were understood in the context of the history of ancient Israel. If psalms spoke of Israel or Jerusalem surrounded by enemies, they were referred to the known crises of Israel's history, especially the siege of Jerusalem in 701 B.C. by the Assyrian king Sennacherib. An extreme form of this approach connected some, or even all of the psalms with events of the Maccabaean revolt and the rule of the Hasmonaean dynasty (169–63 B.C.).

In the present century, psalm studies have been dominated by the form-critical and cultic interpretations. The former, associated with the German, Hermann Gunkel, sought to classify the psalms into types according to their formal structure, and then to suggest a context in the religious life of Israel for the types. The latter, associated with the Norwegian, Sigmund Mowinckel, attempted to reconstruct the worship of the Jerusalem temple, especially as it centred around the king, and it was based on material about worship among ancient Israel's neighbours, as well as upon allusions in the psalms themselves. Subsequent scholarship has criticized these pioneering efforts. Gunkel's psalm types have been considerably modified, and doubt has been cast on the validity of some of Mowinckel's reconstructions. However, the work of these scholars has left a permanent mark on the interpretation of the psalms. Classification of psalms into types on the basis of their formal pattern or structure may be subjective, and unconsciously use content as well as form; but it is useful to consider as a group the so-called individual laments (e.g.

Pss. 3–7, 13–14, 17, 22, 25–26), the psalms of the kingship of God (Pss. 47, 93, 96–99), or the psalms of Zion (Pss. 46, 48, 76, 84, 87, 122), to name only three groups. Also, attempts to reconstruct the worship of the Jerusalem temple have drawn attention to important features of ancient Israelite religion, such as the role of the king, and the covenant between God and the house of David.

No commentator, then, can fail to be indebted to the form-critical and cultic approaches to the psalms; but the usefulness of the approaches can be exaggerated. For example, to label a psalm as an individual lament is sometimes to say nothing that could not be observed by an intelligent reader, and further, if psalms are tied too closely to a particular suggested 'original setting', this may obscure the fact that the psalms were certainly reinterpreted within the Old Testament period, and seen in a fuller perspective in later Jewish and Christian interpretation. Also, concentration on the 'original setting' may sometimes make it difficult for the reader to regard a particular psalm as anything more than interesting information about obsolete ceremonies from a remote and alien culture.

In the present commentary, the writers have tried to strike a balance between the spiritual, historical, form-critical and cultic approaches, seeing value in each where appropriate. The writers have also tried to bring out the religious teaching of permanent value which they believe the psalms to contain.

THE CHARACTER OF THE N.E.B. TRANSLATION

For the translator of the Old Testament, the psalms present some major difficulties. First, it is often not clear from a given psalm what exactly it is about; it may be open to two or more interpretations depending on how a difficult Hebrew word or phrase is regarded. Sometimes, the translator will translate a psalm according to a general view of its meaning which he has arrived at not so much by looking at the psalm as a whole, but by studying the difficult Hebrew word or phrase, and comparing it with similar phrases elsewhere in the Old Testament or in ancient Near Eastern literature. Alternatively, he may let the content of the psalm as a whole override the way in which he translates a difficult word or phrase. In such cases, translators will not claim absolute certainty for their translation; it will represent the best that they feel they can do in a difficult case.

A second reason for the difficulty in translating the psalms arises from the use and re-use of the psalms in Old Testament times, and later in the synagogue and in the church. The psalms can be understood at so many different levels that really adequate translation is impossible. One result of this is that translations of the psalms have different characters, depending on the general approach adopted by their translators. If one compares Ps. 84 in the N.E.B., the Authorized Version and the Psalter of the Book of Common Prayer, the different characters of these renderings are clearly apparent. The Prayer Book version, dating from 1540, preserves some of the early Christian Greek and Latin interpretations of the psalms, with modifications from continental Reformation sources. It presents Ps. 84 as a description of worship and pilgrimage in such a way that the earthly Jerusalem about which the psalm speaks is a veiled symbol for the heavenly Jerusalem, and the pilgrimage to Zion is a symbol for that pilgrimage which is the whole of the religious life of an individual. The Authorized Version is much more literal, and in its attempt to give a faithful rendering of the Hebrew, it sometimes produces nonsense, as in verse 5, where it has 'Blessed is the man whose strength is in thee; in whose heart are the ways of them.' On a superficial reading, the Authorized Version conveys less than the Prayer Book version. The N.E.B. adopts the view that the psalm was sung in connection with a pilgrimage to Zion in ancient Israel. It achieves a consistency of interpretation with the occasional help of a radical treatment of the Hebrew text, but unlike the Prayer Book version, allows no hints that the psalm could be seen in a wider perspective.

The difference between these translations of Ps. 84 is not that one is more 'correct' than the others. At one or two points, the N.E.B. is doubtless more correct from the point of view of Hebrew than the Prayer Book version, but at the same time the N.E.B. contains some conjectures that are at best only possibilities. The proper way to assess a translation is to examine it in the light of its overall approach, and in the case of the N.E.B., this approach seems to have been to render the psalms according to what the translators believed to be the setting of individual psalms in the life of ancient Israel.

Because in the present commentary the writers have sought to see the psalms in a wider perspective than their suggested original setting in ancient Israel, they have regarded the N.E.B. as a witness to the original Hebrew, but they have felt free to criticize the N.E.B. translation, and to draw attention to more traditional approaches to interpretation, where they have felt that the N.E.B. implies too narrow a view, or a misleading interpretation.

LITERARY AND POETIC CHARACTERISTICS
OF THE PSALMS

The psalms are poetry, and they employ several literary devices. Some of these characteristics are apparent, even in translation. Nine psalms, 9–10, 25, 34, 37, 111, 112, 119 and 145, are acrostic psalms, in which individual lines or verses, or groups of verses, begin with successive letters of the Hebrew alphabet. Possibly, the psalmists regarded Hebrew as a special language because in it God had allowed his law and the record of his mighty deeds to be written. The alphabet perhaps symbolized the whole of the Hebrew language, and so, in composing psalms in which verses began with each successive letter of the alphabet, the psalmists were reminding themselves of the marvellous fact that the oracles of God had been recorded in Hebrew. The acrostic principle is at its most elaborate in Ps. 119, where each group of eight verses begins with a successive letter of the alphabet.

In some psalms, refrains can be noticed. In Pss. 42–43 the refrain

> 'How deep I am sunk in misery,
> groaning in my distress:
> yet I will wait for God;
> I will praise him continually,
> my deliverer, my God'

occurs at 42: 5, 11; 43: 5. In Ps. 46: 7, 11 the refrain

> 'The LORD of Hosts is with us,
> the God of Jacob our high stronghold'

is found. Refrains such as that in Ps. 46 and at 80: 3, 7, 19 suggest that they were congregational responses, while in Ps. 136, the fact that every second line is

> 'his love endures for ever'

suggests that this psalm, at least, was used antiphonally, perhaps with the congregation responding every other line with the refrain. In an ancient Hebrew manuscript discovered in caves near the Dead Sea, Ps. 145 appears with a refrain after each verse.

Hebrew poetry is not characterized by rhyme, but by stress and sense. Unfortunately, we do not know how Hebrew was pronounced in biblical times, and what is written in the commentaries about stress must inevitably rest a good deal upon conjecture. In any case, no translation can reproduce the stress in the Hebrew. The sense aspect of Hebrew poetry can, however, be recognized in translation. Often, the sense of a line is exactly reproduced in the next line:

> 'what is man that thou shouldst remember him,
> mortal man that thou shouldst care for him?' (8: 4)

> 'O LORD, who may lodge in thy tabernacle?
> Who may dwell on thy holy mountain?' (15: 1)

Sometimes, the sense of the first line is taken up and slightly expanded in the second:

'The LORD is righteous in his acts;
he brings justice to all who have been wronged' (103:6)

or the sense of the first line may be followed by an opposite sense:

'The LORD watches over the way of the righteous,
but the way of the wicked is doomed.'   (1:6)

Another device is for the sense to be repeated, until it reaches a climax:

'O LORD, the ocean lifts up, the ocean lifts up its clamour;
the ocean lifts up its pounding waves.
Mightier far than the noise of great waters, than the breakers of the sea,
Is the LORD who is on high.'   (93:3f. The N.E.B. is here adapted to follow the order of the Hebrew more closely.)

Sometimes, the poetry employs metaphor:

'A herd of bulls surrounds me,
great bulls of Bashan beset me.
Ravening and roaring lions
open their mouths wide against me' (22:12f.)

or simile:

'I am like a desert-owl in the wilderness,
an owl that lives among ruins,
Thin and meagre, I wail in solitude,
like a bird that flutters on the roof-top.'   (102:6f.)

These are just some examples of the literary and poetic devices that are used in the Psalter, and the psalms can be much better appreciated if we bear them in mind as we read the biblical text. The psalms are religious texts, but their writers were literary craftsmen. They not only strove to find the best possible language in which to utter their prayers and praises; they also probably appreciated that poetry alone was the medium in which it was possible to come closest to the task of expressing the unspeakable mysteries of God in the language of men.

THE CONTENTS OF THE PSALTER

(Some psalms appear under more than one heading. This usually means that they are adaptable for use in different situations, but occasionally it means that the psalm's interpretation is open to debate.)

A. *Hymns*

In praise of God for what he is, good, loving, faithful, etc.: 100, 103, 111, 113, 145, 146, 150.

To God the creator: 8, 19, 24, 29, 104.

To God the bounteous provider: 65, 84, 144, 147.

To the Lord of Israel's history: 68, 78, 105, 111, 114, 117.

To God both as creator and as Lord of history: 33, 89, 95, 135, 136, 144, 148.

To God the mighty, the victorious: 68, 76, 149.

On the final victory of God and his people: 46, 47, 48, 68, 93, 96, 97, 98, 99.

'The LORD is king': 47, 93, 96, 97, 98, 99.

'Songs of Zion' (cp. 137: 3): 46, 48, 76, 84, 87, 122.

Suitable for use by pilgrims: 84, 121, 122, 125, 127.

B. *National psalms*

Prayers for deliverance or victory: 44, 60, 74, 79, 80, 83, 85, 89, 108, 126, 129, 137, 144.

Prayers for blessing and continued protection: 67, 115, 125.

General prayers for mercy or restoration: 90, 106, 123.

Psalms that call the people to obedience: 81, 95.

Royal psalms: 2, 18, 20, 21, 45, 72, 89, 101, 110, 132.

Other psalms that include prayers for the king: 61, 63, 80, 84.
Other psalms that make reference to the king: 78, 122, 144.

C. *Prayers of the individual in time of need*

For protection, deliverance or vindication in the face of
    persecution: 3, 5, 7, 12, 17, 25, 35, 40, 41, 54, 55, 56, 57,
    59, 64, 70, 86, 120, 123, 140, 141, 142, 143.
For use in time of suffering and dereliction: 6, 13, 22, 28, 31,
    38, 39, 42–43, 69, 71, 77, 88, 102, 143.
For justice or personal vindication: 7, 17, 26, 35, 69, 94, 109.
For forgiveness: 6, 25, 38, 51, 130.
Expressing a deep longing for the nearness of God: 22, 25,
    27, 38, 42, 51, 61, 63, 73, 77, 84, 130, 143.
Expressing confidence or trust: 4, 11, 16, 23, 27, 52, 62, 91,
    121, 131.
Suitable for use in a night vigil: 5, 17, 22, 27, 30, 46, 57, 59,
    63, 108, 143.
The 'Penitential Psalms' in Christian tradition: 6, 32, 38,
    51, 102, 130, 143.

D. *Thanksgiving psalms*

For national deliverance: 118 (?), 124.
For personal deliverance: 18, 30, 34, 66, 116, 118, 138.
For forgiveness: 32.
For the knowledge of God's continuing love and care: 92, 107.
See also above: A. *Hymns.*

E. *Psalms giving instruction or containing meditations on various themes*

On the Law: 1, 19, 119.
On the qualities required in the citizens of God's kingdom:
    15, 24, 101, 112.
On corruption in society: 11, 12, 14, 53, 55, 58, 82, 94.
On the lot of mankind, the problem of evil and suffering, the
    ways of the godly and the wicked: 1, 9–10, 14, 36, 37,
    39, 49, 52, 53, 58, 62, 73, 90, 92, 94, 112.

On God's judgement: 50, 75, 82.
On God's blessings: 127, 128, 133.
On God's omniscience: 139.

F. *Psalms generally accounted Messianic in Christian interpretation*

The royal Messiah: 2, 18, 20, 21, 45, 61, 72, 89, 110, 118, 132.
The suffering Messiah: 22, 35, 41, 55, 69, 109.
The second Adam, fulfiller of human destiny: 8, 16, 40.
Psalms describing God as king, creator, etc., applied to Jesus
in the New Testament: 68, 97, 102.

G. *Special categories*

Acrostics: 9–10, 25, 34, 37, 111, 112, 119, 145.
Songs of ascent: 120–134.
Hallel: 113–118.
Hallelujah: 146–150.

✼   ✼   ✼   ✼   ✼   ✼   ✼   ✼   ✼   ✼   ✼   ✼   ✼   ✼

BOOK 4 (*cont.*)

I WILL HAVE NO DEALINGS WITH EVIL

101

I sing of loyalty and justice;   1
I will raise a psalm to thee, O LORD.[a]

I will follow a wise and blameless course,   2
whatever may befall me.[b]
I will go about my house in purity of heart.
I will set before myself no sordid aim;   3
I will hate disloyalty, I will have none of it.
I will reject all crooked thoughts;   4
    I will have no dealings with evil.

[a] I sing ... O LORD: *or* I will follow a course of justice and loyalty; I
will hold thee in awe, O LORD.
[b] whatever may befall me: *prob. rdg.; Heb.* when comest thou to me?

5 I will silence those who spread tales behind men's
        backs,
   I will not sit at table with proud, pompous men,
6 I will choose the most loyal for my companions;
   my servants shall be men whose lives are blameless.
7 No scandal-monger shall live in my household;
   no liar shall set himself up where I can see him.
8 Morning after morning I will put all wicked men to
        silence
   and will rid the LORD's city of all evildoers.

* The speaker of the psalm in its original setting was almost
certainly the king. Verses 2–4 are a statement of the king's
ideals for his personal standards of loyalty to God, and verses
5–8 describe something of how he views his relationship with
his subjects. The psalm could well have been used at the king's
coronation, and thereafter at appropriate festivals. Although it
emphasizes that the king exercised justice on God's behalf
(verse 8), the modern reader cannot help missing the element
of compassion and understanding for those whose lives fall
below the high standards demanded. However, the people
who are by implication condemned in verses 5, 7f. are not
ordinary sinners, but deliberate and persistent wrongdoers,
who would have no appreciation of compassion and understanding if these were offered to them.

   1. *loyalty and justice:* either the loyalty which God has
shown to the king and to the house of David, and the execution of justice which God has entrusted to the king (see N.E.B.
footnote); or it may be the king's loyalty (verses 2–4), and
his execution of justice (verses 5, 7–8).

   2. *whatever may befall me:* the Hebrew 'when wilt thou
come to me?' if correct, is a prayer for closer fellowship with
God. The N.E.B. is based on one of several possible ways of
emending the text. 'Truth will come to me' is a possibility

favoured by a number of interpreters. *go about my house:* although *house* most naturally means the palace and the court, the reference may also be to the king's private, and even solitary, life.

3. *no sordid aim:* Hebrew 'a word (or thing) of Belial'. Belial probably means 'worthlessness', but see Ps. 41: 8 where the N.E.B. connects this same Hebrew phrase with evil spells.

4. *crooked thoughts:* Hebrew 'a twisted (or perverted) heart'. 'Heart' in Hebrew can often be rendered 'mind' or 'thoughts' in English. Here, the crooked thoughts which the king vows to shun would spring from a perversion of the will and character of a person.

5. *spread tales behind men's backs:* this form of slander allows no right of defence by the accused, and is thus to be condemned. *proud, pompous men:* the Hebrew also implies that such men are arrogant and disdainful of others.

6. The king will choose his officials and companions from those who share his personal standards of loyalty to God. At the very least, this will constitute a court and government scrupulously fair in its dealings with the people.

7. The exclusion of scandal-mongers and liars from the king's household will ensure that no Israelite is judged in his absence by those in power.

8. Justice will be administered daily, where necessary, by the king. The open determination of the king to punish wickedness will make God's city holy, as befits the chosen city of God. *

THY YEARS LAST THROUGH ALL GENERATIONS

102

* The psalm falls into three clearly-defined sections: (a) verses 1–11, a prayer to God for deliverance; (b) verses 12–22, a confident declaration that God will restore Jerusalem and that he is one who sets free those who are oppressed; (c) verses

23–8, a renewal of the prayer for help, passing into an assertion of God's eternal nature which will endure when the material world has passed away. Some scholars have argued that verses 12–22 were originally a separate psalm, and it must be admitted that the transitions from verse 11 to verse 12, and from verse 22 to verse 23, are abrupt. In its present form, the psalm is best understood as the prayer of an individual Israelite who sees an analogy between his own plight and that of Jerusalem. Jerusalem is in ruins, but God will restore it; the psalmist is in distress and God will deliver him. To this end, the psalmist makes his plea to the God who is eternal, the psalmist being weak and transient. The traditional Hebrew title of the psalm is 'A prayer of the afflicted when he is overwhelmed, and pours out his complaint before the LORD'. Most interpreters assign the psalm to the period of the Babylonian exile. In Christian use, this is one of the Penitential psalms. ✳

1   LORD, hear my prayer
    and let my cry for help reach thee.
2   Hide not thy face from me
    when I am in distress.
    Listen to my prayer
    and, when I call, answer me soon;
3   for my days vanish like smoke,
    my body is burnt up as in an oven.*a*
4   I am stricken, withered like grass;
    I cannot find the strength to eat.
5   Wasted away,*b* I groan aloud
    and my skin hangs on my bones.
6   I am like a desert-owl in the wilderness,
    an owl that lives among ruins.

[a] as . . . oven: *or, with one MS., like dried meat.*
[b] Wasted away: *transposed from previous verse.*

Thin and meagre, I wail in solitude,[a]   7
like a bird that flutters[b] on the roof-top.
My enemies insult me all the day long;   8
mad with rage, they conspire against me.
I have eaten ashes for bread   9
and mingled tears with my drink.
   In thy wrath and fury   10
     thou hast taken me up and flung me aside.
My days decline as the shadows lengthen,   11
and like grass I wither away.

✦ 2. *Hide not thy face:* it is not implied that this is what God has done, but that this is how it appears to the psalmist.

3. *vanish like smoke:* pass away quickly, with no alleviation of the distress. *my body is burnt up:* literally 'my bones are burnt like a burning mass'. Some interpreters suggest that a description of fever throughout the bodily frame is used as a figure for the psalmist's plight. The N.E.B. seems to imply that the psalmist is as good as dead. The Hebrew word rendered 'oven' is obscure, and see N.E.B. footnote.

6. *desert owl . . . owl:* whatever the precise identification of these birds they are probably unclean creatures to be avoided by Israelites (Lev. 11: 13–19) and solitary; they are a fitting way of describing the psalmist in his distress.

9. The verse may be literally true, i.e. the ashes that adorned the psalmist as a sign of grief and the tears that he shed mingled with his food and drink; but it is more likely to be figurative of distress.

10. *In thy wrath and fury:* some translations take 10*a* closely with verse 9: 'I have mingled tears with my drink because of thy wrath and fury; for thou hast taken me up.' This softens

[a] in solitude: *so Pesh.; Heb. om.*
[b] that flutters: *so some MSS.; others* in solitude.

the sense slightly, but there remains the psalmist's view that
his misfortune is God's punishment.

11. *as the shadows: as* is ambiguous; the sense is that the
psalmist's life is like a lengthening evening shadow that shows
that the day is almost over, i.e. that his life is close to its end. ✳

12 But thou, LORD, art enthroned for ever
    and thy fame shall be known to all generations.
13 Thou wilt arise and have mercy on Zion;
    for the time is come[a] to pity her.
14   Her very stones are dear to thy servants,
    and even her dust moves them with pity.
15 Then shall the nations revere thy name, O LORD,
    and all the kings of the earth thy glory,
16   when the LORD builds up Zion again
    and shows himself in his glory.
17   He turns to hear the prayer of the destitute
    and does not scorn them when they pray.
18 This shall be written down for future generations,
    and a people yet unborn shall praise the LORD.
19 The LORD looks down from his sanctuary on high,
    from heaven he surveys the earth
20   to listen to the groaning of the prisoners
    and set free men under sentence of death;
21 so shall the LORD's name be on men's lips in Zion
    and his praise shall be told in Jerusalem,
22   when peoples are assembled together,
    peoples and kingdoms, to serve the LORD.

✳ 12. *enthroned for ever:* a contrast not only with the psalmist's
transience, but perhaps also a contrast between God's eternal

[a] *Prob. rdg.; Heb. adds* season.

kingship and Jerusalem's disrupted monarchy. *thy fame:* what God has done in past saving acts.

13. *the time is come:* a theme in prophecy; cp. Isa. 40: 2; Jer. 29: 10, which is an occasion of hope for those who look for God's salvation.

14. The intense longing that God's loyal servants have for a return even to ruined Jerusalem will move God to compassion.

15. God's act of restoration will lead foreign kings and nations to *revere thy name*, a theme developed in Isa. 40–55, e.g. Isa. 49: 7. *thy glory:* God's character manifested in his act of redemption.

16f. The tenses of the Hebrew verbs cannot be determined for certain, neither is the connection of these verses together, and with what precedes, certain. It is possible to make verses 16f. the condition of verse 15: the nations will revere God's name when he *builds up Zion* and when he *turns to hear the prayer of the destitute.* The N.E.B. takes the perfect tense of verse 17 not as a prophetic perfect, but as referring to what is always true.

18. The problem here is what the *This* refers to. Some render the passage 'Let this be written down...: that the LORD looks down...' Others refer *This* to what precedes in verses 13–17. Most likely, the reference is to the fact that God will have restored Jerusalem after the exile.

19–22. God's continuing rule from heaven is the best guarantee that in the near future his government of the whole world will be exercised through the mediation of a restored Jerusalem. Although the return from exile was a disappointing event, the Old Testament often merges its conviction of the coming of God's effective universal rule with events that are immediately looked forward to.   *

My strength is broken in mid course;   23
    the time allotted me is short.   24

     Snatch me not away before half my days are done,
     for thy years last through all generations.

25   Long ago thou didst lay the foundations of the earth,
        and the heavens were thy handiwork.
26 They shall pass away, but thou endurest;
        like clothes they shall all grow old;
            thou shalt cast them off like a cloak,
            and they shall vanish;
27 but thou art the same and thy years shall have no end;
28   thy servants' children shall continue,
     and their posterity shall be established in thy presence.

✳ 23f. The psalmist returns to his lament, and although this is an abrupt transition, perhaps the thought is that the psalmist longs to see Jerusalem restored and prays, 'as Jerusalem is restored, so may I be!'

25-7. The poetry builds up to a magnificent climax expressing the eternity of God and the transience of the natural world. A very similar passage is found in Isa. 51: 6, and in the New Testament, these verses are applied to the son of God 'through whom he created all orders of existence' (Heb. 1: 2; cp. 1: 10-12).

28. Whatever his own fate, the psalmist can at least rest in the hope that God's people will endure and continue, to see what his own eyes may not see. The fact that Ps. 103 follows suggests that we should read both together, and see Ps. 103 as a kind of answer to 102. ✳

BLESS THE LORD, MY SOUL

103

1   Bless the LORD, my soul;
        my innermost heart, bless his holy name.
2   Bless the LORD, my soul,
        and forget none of his benefits.

He pardons all my guilt 3
and heals all my suffering.
He rescues me from the pit of death 4
and surrounds me with constant love,
  with tender affection;
he contents me with all good in the prime of life, 5
and my youth is ever new like an eagle's.

The LORD is righteous in his acts; 6
  he brings justice to all who have been wronged.
He taught Moses to know his way 7
  and showed the Israelites what he could do.
The LORD is compassionate and gracious, 8
  long-suffering and for ever constant;
  he will not always be the accuser 9
  or nurse his anger for all time.
He has not treated us as our sins deserve 10
or requited us for our misdeeds.
For as the heaven stands high above the earth, 11
so his strong love stands high over all who fear
    him.
  Far as east is from west, 12
so far has he put our offences away from us.
  As a father has compassion on his children, 13
so has the LORD compassion on all who fear him.
For he knows how we were made, 14
he knows full well that we are dust.

Man's days are like the grass; 15
he blossoms like the flowers of the field:
a wind passes over them, and they cease to be, 16
and their place knows them no more.

17 But the LORD's love never fails those who fear him;
　　his righteousness never fails their sons and their
　　　　grandsons
18　　who listen to his voice*a* and keep his covenant,
　　who remember his commandments and obey them.

19 The LORD has established his throne in heaven,
　　his kingly power over the whole world.
20　　Bless the LORD, all his angels,
　　creatures of might who do his bidding.
21　　Bless the LORD, all his hosts,
　　his ministers who serve his will.
22　　Bless the LORD, all created things,
　　in every place where he has dominion.

　　Bless the LORD, my soul.

* Ps. 103 is much more of a literary whole than Ps. 102; but it shares certain common themes, such as the transience of man (verses 15f.), the eternal kingship of God (verse 19) and God's compassion towards the afflicted (verses 4, 9f.). Also, like 102, this psalm contains both personal utterance (verses 1–5) and hymnic passages, e.g. verses 6–14. The striking difference between the two psalms is that in 102, the personal utterances are laments, while in 103 they are thanksgivings. Thus Ps. 103 has been described as the fulfilment of the hope expressed in Ps. 102: 13.

Many commentators agree that the psalm was composed after the exile. It is not clear that verses 3–5 indicate that the psalmist had been healed from a severe illness, and that the psalm was a public confession of his recovery, as some have suggested. The phrases of verses 3–5 may just as well be a description of God's continual grace towards man. Although a connection between Pss. 102 and 103 cannot be proved, taken together they constitute a wonderful blend of prayer and

[*a*] who listen to his voice: *transposed from end of verse 20.*

24

praise, of despair and affirmation, appropriate not only to the
Babylonian exile and the return, but to countless other situations in the life of the people of God.

1. *my soul:* the psalmist addresses the intellectual, emotional,
aesthetic and spiritual parts of his being. In verses 3–5, the
psalmist's address to his soul continues (literally 'he pardons all
thy guilt', i.e. the soul's guilt), but the N.E.B. uses the first
person, 'my guilt' etc. for the sake of emphasis. *my innermost
heart:* Hebrew 'my innermost parts'. Emotions are described in
Hebrew by means of words for the internal organs of the body.

3. *all my suffering:* it is not clear how far the word for
'suffering' also denotes specific illness, but 'illness' is part of the
meaning.

4. *He rescues me:* the Hebrew for rescues, *gāʾal*, is connected
with the word *gōʾēl*, a near kinsman whose duty is to avenge
and protect his relative. At Job 19: 25, Job speaks of his
advocate (N.E.B. vindicator), his *gōʾēl*, and in Ruth 4: 6, Boaz
is a *gōʾēl* for Ruth. *pit of death:* misfortune that brings the
psalmist close to death. *surrounds me:* the verb 'surrounds' may
also be taken as denominative from the word 'crown' and
translated 'and crowns me'.

5. *prime of life:* the meaning is uncertain, the older translations having 'mouth'. *prime of life* perhaps goes too far as a
paraphrase of the interpretation 'all my days'. *like an eagle's:*
Isa. 40: 29–31. The eagle was a symbol for rejuvenation.

6. *The LORD is righteous:* the N.E.B. separates 6a too much
from 6b, and perhaps fails to bring out the dynamic force of
righteous here. The verse means 'The LORD performs vindica-
ting acts (i.e. deeds which show his righteousness in action)
and brings justice to all who have been wronged.' These acts
include what is mentioned in verse 7 as well as what God
continues to do for his people.

7. *his way:* Hebrew 'ways', possibly meaning God's laws
and his purposes for Israel.

8f. At Exod. 34: 6, God's name is proclaimed as 'compassionate and gracious, long-suffering, ever constant and true'.

As judge, God does not fail to punish wrong, but he does not *nurse his anger* long after sentence is passed and punishment administered.

10–14. Although the psalmist can confess that *He has not treated us as our sins deserve* this does not mean that God has ignored evil, or treated it as other than it is. He has restored relationships broken on the manward side, by such a blend of justice and mercy that it is man himself who has come to understand more deeply the gravity of his sins, and the compassion of God whose *strong love stands high over all who fear him*, and who knows the weakness of man, who is but *dust*.

15f. The Hebrew could mean in verse 16 that the wind passes over man, and he ceases to be. The N.E.B. by using the plurals *flowers* and *them* takes the reference to be to the grass and the flower of the field, whose transitoriness is an apt figure for that of man.

17f. For the contrast between man's frailty and God's permanence, see Ps. 102: 11f., 23, 28.

19. Cp. Ps. 102: 12.

20. *all his angels, creatures of might:* God's servants and messengers who constitute his court and *who do his bidding* in the world.

21. *all his hosts:* possibly including the stars and the heavenly bodies.

22. *all created things:* because God's creation is good (Gen. 1: 31) the psalmist can call upon *all created things* to praise their creator for his goodness. Thus the seen and unseen worlds join together in the praise which this psalm expresses. This theme is more fully developed in Ps. 104. ✻

THOU HAST MADE ALL BY THY WISDOM

104

✻ Whether or not Pss. 103 and 104 are by the same author, as is the opinion of some commentators, Ps. 104 takes up and enlarges the call at 103: 22 for all created things to praise God. However, the main theme of Ps. 104 is that of *dependence* – the dependence of the created order upon God, not merely for its origin, but for its continued life. Man, beast, bird and sea-creature are all dependent on God for their day-to-day sustenance, which, however, God provides through regular, ordered and manifold channels.

The psalm raises the question whether the Israelites possessed a concept of 'nature' as an organized system, and scholars often give a negative answer. Yet it is clear that Israelites saw some events as 'miraculous', that is, as not belonging to what was normally known and experienced (e.g. I Kings 17: 14–16, 17–24). They must have possessed a great deal of knowledge about cause and effect in matters of technology and agriculture. Ps. 104 emphasizes the dependence of all creatures upon God; but this very fact suggests regularity in nature, due to the 'boundaries' that God has set (verses 5, 9).

Another question is whether the psalmist is aware of the dark side of the natural world – 'nature red in tooth and claw'. The Old Testament is aware of what we call natural disasters, such as floods and earthquakes, and these are seen as instruments of God's judgement in the world. Also, at Isa. 11: 6–9, there is a vision of the natural world transformed. But it is unfair to expect the psalmist to say everything in one psalm. Ps. 104 is a wonderful Israelite expression of the wonders of nature and their dependence upon God. It may be related in some way to the wider ancient Near Eastern tradition on this theme, especially to the *Hymn to Aten* (J. B. Pritchard, *Ancient Near Eastern Texts*, pp. 369f.) an Egyptian text from the years 1380–1362 B.C.

> e.g. 'How manifold it is, what thou hast made!
> They are hidden from the face (of man).
> O sole god, like whom there is no other!
> Thou didst create the world according to thy desire,
> Whilst thou wert alone:

> All men, cattle, and wild beasts,
> Whatever is on earth, going upon (its) feet,
> And what is on high, flying with its wings.'

But the psalm is a masterpiece in its own right. ✳

1   Bless the Lord, my soul:
  O Lord my God, thou art great indeed,
    clothed in majesty and splendour,
2   and wrapped in a robe of light.
    Thou hast spread out the heavens like a tent
3   and on their waters laid the beams of thy pavilion;
    who takest the clouds for thy chariot,
    riding on the wings of the wind;
4   who makest the winds thy messengers
    and flames of fire thy servants;
5   thou didst fix the earth on its foundation
    so that it never can be shaken;
6   the deep overspread it like a cloak,
    and the waters lay above the mountains.
7   At thy rebuke they ran,
    at the sound of thy thunder they rushed away,
8   flowing over the hills,
    pouring down into the valleys
    to the place appointed for them.
9 Thou didst fix a boundary which they might not pass;
    they shall not return to cover the earth.

✳ 1–4. The exact relation of the clauses together is not easy to determine, but without emendation, N.E.B. has no support from the Hebrew in taking the first phrase of verse 2 *wrapped in a robe of light* with verse 1 and beginning a new sequence with *Thou hast spread . . .* One possibility is to put a full stop after *great indeed* (verse 1), continuing 'Thou art *clothed in majesty* . . .' These opening verses describe the smallness of the world in relation to God, by picturing light as God's robe, the heavens as his tent, clouds as his chariot and so on. In verses 2–4, the use of the participles in the Hebrew suggests God's continuing involvement in his creation. The cosmology implied here is that common in the ancient Near East (cp. Gen. 1 and Ps. 18).

who makest the winds: in Hebrew 'wind' can also mean 'spirit' and 'messenger' can also mean 'angel', hence the Authorized Version's 'who maketh his angels spirits'. The N.E.B. suggests, rightly, that such is God's command of nature that he performs his will through the natural media of wind and fire. Verse 4 is quoted in Heb. 1: 7.

5–9. Many interpreters (against N.E.B.) begin a new section here, which describes God's *work* of creation, as opposed to his *relation* to creation in verses 1–4. Verses 5–9 seem to be an expanded account of Gen. 1: 2, 9–10. The earth unmovably fixed *on its foundation*, was covered by *the deep* (Gen. 1: 2), i.e. the primaeval waters. At God's command (Gen. 1: 9) the waters went to their appointed places, never to *return to cover the earth* (cp. Gen. 9: 11). It is possible that in verse 8 the subjects of the verbs are the hills and the valleys ('the hills rose, the valleys sank down'), but N.E.B. gives a graphic rendering of the Hebrew. ✶

Thou dost make springs break out in the gullies,   10
    so that their water runs between the hills.
The wild beasts all drink from them,   11
    the wild asses quench their thirst;
the birds of the air nest on their banks   12
    and sing among the leaves.

From thy high pavilion thou dost water the hills;   13
    the earth is enriched by thy provision.

�֞ 10–13. God's provision by means of water.

10. *springs break out in the gullies:* a permanent supply of water from springs, as opposed to seasonal rains flowing along *wadi* beds. The latter are little use in the dry summer season to thirsty creatures. In verses 5–9 God's *control* of the waters is described; in this verse, it is his *gift* of waters.

12. *nest on their banks:* i.e. in the trees that grow along their banks. �֞

14   Thou makest grass grow for the cattle
        and green things for those who toil for man,
     bringing bread out of the earth
15   and wine to gladden men's hearts,
     oil to make their faces shine
     and bread to sustain their strength.
16   The trees of the LORD are green and leafy,
        the cedars of Lebanon which he planted;
17   the birds build their nests in them,
     the stork makes her home in their tops.[a]
18   High hills are the haunt of the mountain-goat,
     and boulders a refuge for the rock-badger.

✖ 14–18. God's provision by means of what grows.

14. *for those who toil for man:* refers to the animals that work for man. Another possible rendering is 'plants for men to cultivate' (Revised Standard Version). *bringing bread:* i.e. corn that will be made into bread.

16. *The trees of the LORD:* the purpose of these may be not only to provide a home for birds (verse 17), but numerous things for man's life; also the *cedars of Lebanon* are an awesome part of creation.

18. Even the barren *High hills* and *boulders* have their purpose in God's design, as they provide homes for some animals. ✖

[a] in their tops: *prob. rdg.; Heb.* the pine-trees.

Thou hast made the moon to measure the year   19
and taught the sun where to set.

When thou makest darkness and it is night,   20
all the beasts of the forest come forth;
the young lions roar for prey,   21
seeking their food from God.

When thou makest the sun rise, they slink away   22
and go to rest in their lairs;
but man comes out to his work   23
and to his labours until evening.

✻ 19–23. God's provision by means of the alternation of day and night.

19. *the moon:* the year was a lunar year in ancient Israel, periodically corrected to accord with the position of the sun. *the sun:* regulates day and night.

20–2. Even during the hours of darkness, God is still attending to his creation, as he feeds nocturnal animals.

23. Man, however, is provided for in the dignity of *his work* and *his labours.* ✻

Countless are the things thou hast made, O LORD.   24
Thou hast made all by thy wisdom;
and the earth is full of thy creatures,
beasts great and small.   25

Here is the great immeasurable sea,
in which move creatures beyond number.
Here ships sail to and fro,   26
here is Leviathan whom thou hast made thy plaything.[a]

✻ 24–6. An expression of wonder at God's manifold creation.
24. *by thy wisdom:* the creation in every aspect is a mani-

[a] thy plaything: *or* that it may sport in it.

festation of God's wisdom. At Prov. 8: 22–31, it is said that the
world was created by means of wisdom, which is personified.

   25. the great immeasurable sea: was a particular source of awe
and wonder. Leviathan (verse 26) is taken by the N.E.B. at
Job 41: 1 to be a whale, and this may be the sense here. In
Canaanite literature Leviathan is a seven-headed monster, and
a sinister force. We do not know how far this view of
Leviathan was known in later Israel. Compared with the
Canaanite view, Leviathan has been reduced to a plaything in
the Old Testament. See also on Ps. 74: 13f. ✴

27   All of them look expectantly to thee
        to give them their food at the proper time;
28   what thou givest them they gather up;
        when thou openest thy hand, they eat their fill.
29   Then thou hidest thy face, and they are restless and
                troubled;
        when thou takest away their breath, they fail
        [and they return to the dust from which they came];
30   but when thou breathest into them, they recover;
        thou givest new life to the earth.

   ✴ 27–30. The complete dependence of all creatures upon God.
   27. All of them: most likely the creatures, including man,
referred to in verses 10–26.
   29. [and they return to the dust . . .]: the N.E.B. bracket
implies that the line is a gloss, suggesting that creatures die
(*return to the dust*) and are then restored to life. However, the
text may equally well be understood as reflecting the transience
of life and the replacing of each old generation by a new
generation. ✴

31   May the glory of the LORD stand for ever
        and may he rejoice in his works!
32   When he looks at the earth, it quakes;

when he touches the hills, they pour forth smoke.

I will sing to the LORD as long as I live,   33
all my life I will sing psalms to my God.
May my meditation please the LORD,   34
as I show my joy in him!
Away with all sinners from the earth   35
and may the wicked be no more!

Bless the LORD, my soul.

    O praise the LORD.[a]

✻ 31–5. Concluding prayers and vows.

31f. The psalmist reminds us that God is not wholly benign
in the way that men would like him to be. The creator can just
as easily destroy his creation (verse 32) and the psalmist prays
that God may not have occasion to do this.

33–5. The contemplation of the wonderful natural order is
not to be an aesthetic pleasure only. It must result in action,
including praise, meditation, and right conduct. God's world
is spoilt most of all by the sins of men. Thus the psalmist not
only prays *may the wicked be no more:* by implication he pledges
his obedience to God's law and will. ✻

THINK UPON ALL HIS WONDERS

105

✻ Ps. 105 gives an account of the history of Israel from the
time of Abraham to the occupation of the promised land. This
last happening (verse 44) is a fulfilment of a promise to Jacob
(verse 11) (although the promise was first made to Abraham),
and thus the history is presented in such a way as to show how
through many vicissitudes, God was working out the plan
which his promise implied. The users of the psalm are exhorted
to 'think upon' these, and other 'wonders' (verse 2), and to

[a] O praise the LORD: *Heb.* Hallelujah.

pledge that obedience to God's 'laws' and 'statutes' (verse 45) which was the purpose of God's choosing of Israel.

Verses 1–15 of the psalm are used, together with Ps. 96 and Ps. 106: 1, 47f., in the account of David bringing the Ark to Jerusalem in 1 Chron. 16, and although it is not *a priori* impossible that the psalm is as old as this, most scholars date it in the period after the exile. An important question is whether the psalm is dependent on the Pentateuch in something like its final form. If this were so, then the psalm would certainly have been composed after the exile; but it is also possible that, whether late or early, it draws on an independent hymnic tradition of Israel's history. In any case, it is an important witness to the method of interpreting history in ancient Israel. The permanent value of the psalm is that it invites us to think upon the whole disclosure of divine purpose for the world. ✻

1[a] Give the LORD thanks and invoke him by name,
  make his deeds known in the world around.
2 Pay him honour with song and psalm
  and think upon all his wonders.
3 Exult in his hallowed name;
  let those who seek the LORD be joyful in heart.
4 Turn to the LORD, your strength,[b]
  seek his presence always.
5 Remember the wonders that he has wrought,
  his portents and the judgements he has given,
6 O offspring of Abraham his servant, O chosen sons of
  Jacob.

7 He is the LORD our God;
  his judgements fill the earth.
8 He called to mind his covenant from long ago,[c]

[a] *Verses 1–15: cp. 1 Chr. 16: 8–22.*
[b] your strength: *lit.* and his strength.   [c] from long ago: *or* for ever.

34

the promise he extended to a thousand generations –
  the covenant made with Abraham,   9
  his oath given to Isaac,
the decree by which he bound himself for Jacob,   10
his everlasting covenant with Israel:
'I will give you the land of Canaan', he said,   11
  'to be your possession, your patrimony.'
  A small company it was,   12
few in number, strangers in that land,
roaming from nation to nation,   13
from one kingdom to another;
but he let no one ill-treat them,   14
for their sake he admonished kings:
  'Touch not my anointed servants,   15
  do my prophets no harm.'

He called down famine on the land   16
and cut short their daily bread.[a]
But he had sent on a man before them,   17
Joseph, who was sold into slavery;
he was kept a prisoner with fetters on his feet   18
and an iron collar clamped on his neck.
He was tested by the LORD's command   19
until what he foretold came true.
Then the king sent and set him free,   20
  the ruler of nations released him;
he made him master of his household   21
  and ruler over all his possessions,
to correct his officers at will   22
  and teach his counsellors wisdom.

[a] and cut . . . bread: *lit.* and broke their stick of bread.

23 Then Israel too went down into Egypt
    and Jacob came to live in the land of Ham.

24 There God made his people very fruitful,
      he made them stronger than their enemies,

25 whose hearts he turned to hatred of his people
      and double-dealing with his servants.

✻ 1. *Give the LORD thanks:* although Israelites are clearly the people exhorted here, we do not know whether a specific occasion or ceremony, such as a covenant renewal ceremony, was the occasion of the psalm.

2. *think upon:* the Hebrew verb can also mean 'talk of', 'declare', and some translations prefer this meaning.

4. *Turn to the LORD:* literally 'seek the LORD and his strength'. The N.E.B. presumably wishes to distinguish the two different verbs in 4a and 4b, both usually rendered 'seek'. *your strength:* the Hebrew (see the N.E.B. footnote) has 'and his strength' which could indicate the Ark as a symbol of God's protecting power; the ancient translators have a verbal form meaning 'and be strong'.

5. *Remember:* i.e. have in continual remembrance. *portents:* a special display of God's power, especially in events such as the plagues, and the miracle at the Red Sea.

6. *O chosen sons:* possibly the Hebrew should be read as 'sons of Jacob his chosen one', a parallel with *Abraham his servant.*

7. *He is the LORD our God:* or perhaps 'He, the LORD, is our God', the emphasis being on *the LORD* as a personal name which signifies his character (cp. Exod. 33:18–19). Because *his judgements fill the earth* the psalmist can proceed to talk about God's deeds on Israel's behalf against the background of the whole world.

8. *He called to mind . . . from long ago:* it is not clear from the N.E.B. at what point in time God *called to mind his covenant,* unless the period of the oppression in Egypt is meant. It may be easier to take *he called to mind* as a perfect expressing a

general truth – he calls to mind. Another difficulty is that *from long ago* should be taken with the verb, and not with *his covenant*. Thus we should perhaps render the verse 'He ever calls to mind . . .' *a thousand generations:* for ever.

9f. An allusion to various passages such as Gen. 12: 2; 28: 13, where a promise is made.

11. There is no exactly corresponding promise in Genesis.

12–15. The wanderings of the patriarchs in Genesis are here summarized, but in a poetic way (and cp. Deut. 26: 5–9). The kings who were *admonished* (verse 14) would be Pharaoh (Gen. 12: 17) and Abimelech (Gen. 20: 3). *anointed servants:* it is unlikely that the patriarchs were anointed. Therefore, either the psalmist incorrectly thought that this was so, or 'anointed' has the weakened sense of 'appointed' here. Abraham is called a prophet at Gen. 20: 7.

16–23 summarize the story of Joseph (Gen. 37, 39–47).

16. *He called down:* Gen. 42: 5.

17. *he had sent on a man:* cp. Gen. 45: 7 'God sent me ahead of you . . .'

18. *an iron collar clamped on his neck:* Hebrew 'his soul entered (into) iron'. It is widely held that the Hebrew word for 'soul' sometimes means 'neck', and the N.E.B. makes good sense and yields a good parallel with 18*a*. However, there are modern defenders of the interpretation that Joseph's 'soul', i.e. his emotional and spiritual life, suffered intensely.

19. *He was tested:* although Joseph was sent ahead by God, his task was not performed without wrongful accusation and suffering. To that extent, Joseph is a suffering servant of God in the Old Testament.

25. *whose hearts he turned:* see Exod. 7: 2–4. The exodus tradition recognizes that although the Egyptian obstinacy in refusing to let Israel go was in some way divinely caused, it was also a human decision (e.g. Exod. 8: 19). ✶

He sent his servant Moses   26
and Aaron whom he had chosen.

27　They were his*a* mouthpiece to announce his signs,
　　　his portents in the land of Ham.

28　He sent darkness, and all was dark,
　　　but still they resisted his commands.

29　He turned their waters into blood
　　　and killed all their fish.

30　Their country swarmed with frogs,
　　　even their princes' inner chambers.

31　At his command came swarms of flies
　　　and maggots the whole land through.

32　He changed their rain into hail
　　　and flashed fire over their country.

33　He blasted their vines and their fig-trees
　　　and splintered the trees throughout the land.

34　At his command came locusts,
　　　hoppers past all number,

35　they consumed every green thing in the land,
　　　consumed all the produce of the soil.

36　Then he struck down all the first-born in Egypt,*b*
　　　the firstfruits of their manhood;

37　he led Israel*c* out, laden with silver and gold,
　　　and among all their tribes no man fell.

38　The Egyptians were glad when they went,
　　　for fear of Israel had taken hold of them.

39　He spread a cloud as a screen,
　　　and fire to light up the night.

40　They asked, and he sent them quails,
　　　he gave them bread from heaven in plenty.

[a] *So Sept.; Heb.* their.
[b] in Egypt: *so some MSS.; others* in their land.
[c] *Lit.* them.

He opened a rock and water gushed out,   41
   a river flowing in a parched land;
    for he had remembered his solemn promise   42
     given to his servant Abraham.
So he led out his people rejoicing,   43
   his chosen ones in triumph.
He gave them the lands of heathen nations   44
and they took possession where others had toiled,
    so that they might keep his statutes   45
    and obey his laws.

   O praise the LORD.

✻ 26–38. Moses and Aaron, the plagues and the exodus. For
verses 26–36, cp. Exod. 7–11.

27. *They were his mouthpiece:* in Exodus, Aaron figures only
in some of the plagues, namely those usually assigned to the
writer called 'P'. (See *Exodus* in this series, pp. 4, 44.) However, Ps. 105 is far from following the P version of the plagues
(darkness, for example, is not a P plague) and it is most likely
that we have here an independent hymnic version of the plagues.

28. *darkness:* the ninth plague (Exod. 10: 21–3). The most
likely reason why Ps. 105 mentions what is normally regarded as
the ninth plague first is that we have an independent tradition.
There is no need to regard the verse as a marginal gloss, nor to
seek theological reasons for this plague coming first.

29. The first plague (Exod. 7: 14–25).

30. The second plague (Exod. 8: 1–15).

31. *flies:* the fourth plague (Exod. 8: 20–32). *maggots:* the
third plague (Exod. 8: 16–19). The identification of the
insects or creatures involved is uncertain.

32–3. *hail:* the seventh plague (Exod. 9: 13–35). *fire:*
cp. Exod. 9: 23.

34–5. The eighth plague (Exod. 10: 1–20).

36. The tenth plague (Exod. 11).

37. *silver and gold:* see Exod. 12: 35–6.

39–41. A summary of the wilderness wanderings, and God's provision during them.

39. *cloud as a screen:* this corresponds with Exod. 14: 19f., where the pillar of cloud prevented contact between the Israelites and the Egyptians. Elsewhere (e.g. Exod. 13: 21f.) the pillars of cloud and fire guided the Israelites on their way.

40f. See Exod. 16–17. *They asked:* no reference is made to the complaining of the Israelites. This theme is more than adequately stressed in Ps. 106. Perhaps *asked* is understood as 'prayed for', 'requested'. The emphasis in the psalm is on God guiding and providing, in accordance with his promises.

42. *his solemn promise:* literally 'his holy promise (word)' a promise backed and guaranteed by God's holy character.

43. *rejoicing . . . triumph:* perhaps an allusion to the Song of Moses, Exod. 15.

44f. God's plan to create a people loyal only to himself, through which the nations of the world could be blessed (cp. verse 1) was only fully realized when the Israelites possessed their own land. There, in peace and security, they were to *keep his statutes and obey his laws.* This was the ideal, to which God's providence was directed. This psalm should not be read in isolation from Ps. 106, for in that psalm we have another presentation of Israelite history, this time interpreted from the angle of Israel's unfaithfulness. Taken together, Pss. 105 and 106 reveal that gulf between God's call and Israel's response which makes the Old Testament incomplete in itself, and needing to be completed by a New Covenant. ✲

WE HAVE SINNED LIKE OUR FOREFATHERS

106

✲ Ps. 105 is an account of the history of Israel in which all the stress is placed on God's faithfulness to his people; here the history is presented to show the people's unfaithfulness to God.

The date of the psalm, on the internal evidence of verses 27
and 47, is most likely to be the period of the exile, though we
cannot be certain whether it was composed and used in
Babylon or Jerusalem. Some interpreters would assign the
psalm to the period after the exile; and it has been suggested
that it was used as part of the liturgy of national confession at a
covenant renewal ceremony. It is possible, although not
certain, that the presentation of the selected events from Israel's
history derives from a knowledge of the Pentateuch in its
completed form. ✳

O praise the LORD.   1

It is good to give thanks to the LORD;
    for his love endures for ever.
Who will tell of the LORD's mighty acts   2
    and make his praises heard?
    Happy are they who act justly   3
    and do right at all times!
Remember me, LORD, when thou showest favour to thy   4
            people,
    look upon me when thou savest them,
    that I may see the prosperity of thy chosen,   5
rejoice in thy nation's joy and exult with thy own
            people.

We have sinned like our forefathers,   6
we have erred and done wrong.
Our fathers in Egypt took no account of thy marvels,   7
    they did not remember thy many acts of faithful love,
    but in spite of all*a* they rebelled by the Red Sea.*b*
    Yet the LORD delivered them for his name's sake   8
    and so made known his mighty power.

[a] in spite of all: *prob. rdg.; Heb. obscure.*   [b] *Or* the Sea of Reeds.

9   He rebuked the Red Sea and it dried up,
  he led his people through the deeps as through the
        wilderness.
10   So he delivered them from those who hated them,
    and claimed them back from the enemy's hand.
11   The waters closed over their adversaries,
    not one of them survived.
12 Then they believed his promises and sang praises to him.

13   But they quickly forgot all he had done
    and would not wait to hear his counsel;
14   their greed was insatiable in the wilderness,
    they tried God's patience in the desert.
15   He gave them what they asked
    but sent a wasting sickness among them.[a]

16   They were envious of Moses in the camp,
    and of Aaron, who was consecrated to the LORD.
17 The earth opened and swallowed Dathan,
    it closed over the company of Abiram;
18   fire raged through their company,
    the wicked perished in flames.

19   At Horeb they made a calf
    and bowed down to an image;
20   they exchanged their Glory[b]
  for the image of a bull that feeds on grass.
21   They forgot God their deliverer,
    who had done great deeds in Egypt,
22   marvels in the land of Ham,
    terrible things at the Red Sea.

[a] among them: *or* in their throats.
[b] their Glory: *or* the glory of God (*cp. Jer.* 2: 11; *Romans* 1: 23).

So his purpose was to destroy them,   23
but Moses, the man he had chosen,
threw himself into the breach
to turn back his wrath lest it destroy them.

☆ 1. *O praise the LORD:* This is the first psalm to begin with
this call, although Pss. 104 and 105 end with it. The phrase
occurs only in books 4 and 5 of the psalms, and it is not known
whether it is a liturgical direction or simply a liturgical phrase.
The Hebrew is often transliterated as 'Hallelujah' = *hallelū* (O
praise) *jāh* (Yahweh, the LORD). *It is good: good* can refer either
to the act of giving thanks (so the N.E.B.) or to God himself
(so the older translations). Applied to the act, it means 'fitting',
'appropriate'. Applied to God, it indicates his graciousness.

2. *Who will tell:* nobody in fact can do this adequately.

3. *Happy are they:* nobody may be able to speak adequately
about 'the LORD's mighty acts', but it remains open to all to
act in accordance with justice and righteousness. Such people
are blessed (see Ps. 119: 1).

4f. *Remember me:* like the psalmist at 89: 46f. and (less
directly) 102: 23f., the psalmist prays that he may live and see
the time *when thou showest favour to thy people,* most naturally
referring to the return from exile, but also capable of reference
to other happenings.

6. *We have sinned:* the psalmist, or the worshipping
community, makes the confession that introduces the sketch of
Israelite history. The confession may be similar to forms that
were used on special occasions (cp. 1 Kings 8: 47) and it is
reminiscent of the confession used in later Judaism on the Day
of Atonement. The incidents that are to be mentioned are
paradigms – examples of a rebellious human nature shared by
the psalmist with his forefathers.

7-12. Rebellion at the Red Sea; see Exod. 14: 10-12.

7. *in spite of all:* reading *'aleyhem* for the Hebrew *'al yām* 'at
the Sea'. Many commentators read *'elyōn* 'the Most High'.

9. *as through the wilderness:* N.E.B. seems to link the leading

through the sea with the wilderness wanderings. Others render 'as through a wilderness' i.e. 'as through dry (desert) ground'.

12. *sang praises:* cp. Exod. 15: 1.

13-15. Rebellion in the wilderness. See Ps. 78: 30f. and the comments thereon.

15. *He gave them . . . but sent a wasting sickness:* in the N.E.B. translation the giving and the punishing are two separate actions. On another interpretation they are the same thing. The story in Num. 11: 4-23, 31-4, has here been spiritualized so as to express the idea that it is a dangerous thing for God to give people what they want if they want it for the wrong reasons.

16-18. Rebellion against Moses and Aaron; cp. Num. 16: 1-35; Deut. 11: 5-7. This was not a general revolt (see Num. 16 but note that Korah is not mentioned in this psalm) but perhaps it expressed a desire to rebel against divinely-decreed order, a desire felt by all people at some time. The rebels argued against Moses and Aaron: 'Every member of the community is holy and the LORD is among them all. Why do you set yourselves up above the assembly of the LORD?' (Num. 16: 3). But the choosing of Moses and the family of Aaron did more than merely confer privilege – it involved them in suffering and intercession on behalf of the people (verses 23, 30, 32f.). Would the rebels have been willing to pay the price of receiving the divine commission?

19-23. Rebellion at Sinai. See Exod. 32 and cp. 1 Kings 12: 28.

19. *At Horeb:* Horeb is an alternative name for Sinai, found, e.g. at Exod. 3: 1. It is doubtful whether we can identify the origin of the psalmist's tradition by this name alone.

20f. *their Glory:* it is impossible to describe God in terms drawn from the natural world; hence the use of 'glory'. It is possible that the original text had 'his glory', but this would not fundamentally affect the sense. *feeds on grass:* a contrast is made between the created object dependent for sustenance on created things, and the deliverer, the Lord of nature, who did *great deeds in Egypt*.

23. *threw himself into the breach:* apparently a military

metaphor, stressing Moses's brave exposure of himself to the
greatest danger on his people's behalf. ✳

They made light of the pleasant land,   24
　　disbelieving his promise;
　　　they muttered treason in their tents   25
and would not obey the LORD.
So with uplifted hand he swore   26
to strike them down in the wilderness,
to scatter their descendants among the nations   ·   27
　　and disperse them throughout the world.

They joined in worshipping the Baal of Peor   28
　　and ate meat sacrificed to lifeless gods.
　　　Their deeds provoked the LORD to anger,   29
and plague broke out amongst them;
but Phinehas stood up and interceded,   30
　　so the plague was stopped.
This was counted to him as righteousness   31
throughout all generations for ever.

They roused the LORD to anger at the waters of Meribah, 32
and Moses suffered because of them;
　　for they had embittered his spirit   33
　　and he had spoken rashly.

They did not destroy the peoples round about,   34
as the LORD had commanded them to do,
　　but they mingled with the nations,   35
　　learning their ways;
　　　they worshipped their idols   36
and were ensnared by them.
　　　Their sons and their daughters   37
　　they sacrificed to foreign demons;

38   they shed innocent blood,
      the blood of sons and daughters
      offered to the gods of Canaan,
   and the land was polluted with blood.

39   Thus they defiled themselves by their conduct
   and they followed their lusts and broke faith with God.

40   Then the LORD grew angry with his people
      and loathed them, his own chosen nation;

41   so he gave them into the hands of the nations,
   and they were ruled by their foes;

42   their enemies oppressed them
      and made them subject to their power.

43   Many times he came to their rescue,
   but they were disobedient and rebellious still.[a]

44   And yet, when he heard them wail and cry aloud,
      he looked with pity on their distress;

45   he called to mind his covenant with them
      and, in his boundless love, relented;

46   he roused compassion for them
      in the hearts of all their captors.

47   Deliver us, O LORD our God,
      and gather us in from among the nations
      that we may give thanks to thy holy name
      and make thy praise our pride.

48   Blessed be the LORD the God of Israel
      from everlasting to everlasting;
   and let all the people say 'Amen.'

     O praise the LORD.

[a] *Prob. rdg.; Heb. adds* and were brought low by their guilt.

✻ 24-7. Rebellion on the threshold of the promised land. See Num. 13, 14. The Israelites were more influenced by the bad report of the promised land brought back by ten of the spies, than by the good report of Joshua and Caleb.

26f. The punishment that the rebellious people (including the innocent Moses) would not be allowed to enter the promised land is here apparently extended to include *their descendents*, i.e. the Babylonian exiles (verse 27).

28-31. Rebellion in Moab. See Num. 25, where, however, we have little explicit information about the exact nature of the apostasy. In this psalm, there is again a contrast between the lifeless gods (verse 28) and the God whose anger caused plague to break out amongst them. *sacrificed to lifeless gods:* is probably a correct paraphrase of the Hebrew 'sacrifices of the dead'. *Phinehas:* the prominence of Phinehas is interesting, and the intercession ascribed to him here contrasts with his bloodthirsty zeal described in Num. 25: 6-13 which says nothing about intercession. This psalm stems from priestly circles; and for references to Phinehas in later literature see 1 Macc. 2: 54 and Ecclus. 45: 23. *counted . . . as righteousness:* see Num. 25: 10f. and cp. Gen. 15: 6.

32f. Rebellion in the wilderness, see Num. 20: 2-13. The psalmist seems to have broken the historical sequence with this incident but we probably have an independent tradition here. The account in Num. 20: 2-13 is far from clear as to how Moses demonstrated his lack of trust in God, for which the punishment was not to lead the people into the promised land. Verses 32f. in this psalm exonerate Moses to some extent.

34-9. Rebellion in the promised land. In 6 verses, the psalmist interprets over 600 years of history in terms of recurring apostasy, from the settlement in Canaan, to the Babylonian exile. If the command to *destroy the peoples round about* (verse 34) seems harsh and barbaric to us, we must remember that from the point of view of hindsight, the mingling of Israel *with the nations* accompanied by *learning their ways* (verse 35) had led to disaster. The worship of false gods led to debased ethical standards, to human sacrifice and unjust killing (verse 38), to prostitution and immorality (verse 39).

40–6. God's judgement upon his people. This passage reminds us particularly of the period of the judges, but probably is meant to be a larger summary of Israel's fortunes, ending with the exile (verse 46).

47. Concluding prayer. This verse connects with verse 6, in dependence upon the conviction that when Israel called in their distress upon God, 'he called to mind his covenant with them and, in his boundless love, relented' (verse 45). Its most natural reference is a prayer for deliverance from the Babylonian exile, and the coming dispersion.

48. Concluding doxology to the fourth book of psalms. See 41: 13; 72: 18f. and 89: 52. ✳

BOOK 5

LET THEM THANK THE LORD FOR HIS
ENDURING LOVE

107

✳ Although Ps. 107 begins the fifth book of the psalms, it cannot be considered in complete isolation from Pss. 105 and 106. It is almost the synthesis of these two contrasting psalms, and can be considered as an elaboration of 106: 43: 'Many times he came to their rescue.' In its present form, it is natural to regard the psalm as having been composed after the exile, with explicit references to deliverance from exile in verses 2f., and allusion to the return from Babylon across the desert in verses 4–7, and to that defeat of Babylon which led to the return, in verses 10–16 (cp. Isa. 45: 2). Some interpreters posit an 'earlier' version, made up of verses 1, 4–32. This contains four sections, each concluded by a doxology, describing the deliverance of travellers, prisoners, sick persons and seafarers. It is suggested that such a psalm would be used as a communal thanksgiving by those who had been delivered. This is a plausible, though not demonstrable, theory. Verses 33–43 do not conform to the preceding structure of the psalm, though it can be argued that verses 33–8 refer back to verses 4–9, and that verse 39 alludes to verses 10–16, by describing the defeat of rulers necessary for the release of prisoners. Common to all sections of the psalm, including verses 33–43, is the idea of reversal of fortunes, dependent on the 'enduring love' of God in response to human need (cp. Luke 1: 51–3). ✻

It is good to give thanks to the LORD,   1
    for his love endures for ever.
So let them say who were redeemed by the LORD,   2
    redeemed by him from the power of the enemy
    and gathered out of every land,   3
from east and west, from north and south.[a]

✻ 1. *It is good:* see on 106: 1.
   2. *So let them say:* So is not in the Hebrew but is necessary for the sense. It is not clear whether the phrase should refer to what immediately precedes, or whether it is to be connected with what follows. The undoubted awkwardness in the Hebrew is an argument for those who see verses 2f. as later insertions, adapting an earlier psalm to use after the exile. The persons *redeemed by the LORD* are most probably exiles who were in Babylon (Isa. 62: 12). ✻

Some lost their way in desert wastes;   4
    they found no road to a city to live in;
   hungry and thirsty,   5
    their spirit sank within them.
So they cried to the LORD in their trouble,   6
    and he rescued them from their distress;

[a] and south: *prob. rdg., cp. Targ.; Heb.* and west.

7 he led them by a straight and easy way
    until they came to a city to live in.
8 Let them thank the LORD for his enduring love
    and for the marvellous things he has done for men:
9 he has satisfied the thirsty
    and filled the hungry with good things.

* 4–9. The deliverance of travellers. The main question here
is the meaning of *a city to live in* (verses 4 and 7). Many commentators hold that it means 'inhabited city' where the lost
travellers could obtain food and shelter, rather than a place to
settle down and live. Verse 36 has the same Hebrew phrase,
however, where it can only mean a permanent home. The
N.E.B. rendering might imply the difficult return from exile
across the desert, or even suggest the wilderness wanderings
after the exodus as in Isa. 35: 8. A more general interpretation
would not be incompatible with these ideas.

7. *straight and easy way: easy* has no equivalent in the Hebrew
though it helps to express the fact that God's intervention
made the journey easy for exhausted people. *

10 Some sat in darkness, dark as death,
    prisoners bound fast in iron,
11 because they had rebelled against God's commands
    and flouted the purpose of the Most High.
12 Their spirit was subdued by hard labour;
    they stumbled and fell with none to help them.
13 So they cried to the LORD in their trouble,
    and he saved them from their distress;
14 he brought them out of darkness, dark as death,
    and broke their chains.
15 Let them thank the LORD for his enduring love

and for the marvellous things he has done for men:
he has shattered doors of bronze, 16
    bars of iron he has snapped in two.

☆ 10-16. *The deliverance of prisoners.*

10. Although verse 16 suggests the defeat of Babylon (Isa.
45: 2), it is not true that all the exiles were *prisoners bound fast in
iron*, though no doubt a minority were (e.g. 2 Kings 25: 28f.).
Once again, specific and general applications are possible. *dark
as death:* this refers to the darkness, not the prisoners. The
Hebrew word (see Ps. 23: 4) indicates a kind of darkness that is
threatening and which removes all hope. *prisoners:* the N.E.B.
rendering of a word traditionally translated as 'affliction'.

11. *because they had rebelled:* the imprisonment is seen as
punishment for disobeying God.

12f. *Their spirit:* Hebrew literally 'heart'. Perhaps their
hopes or that which caused them to disregard God's commands
is meant here. *none to help:* they finally learned not to rely on
their own judgement and strength, but sincerely *cried to the
LORD in their trouble.*

16. *doors of bronze:* cp. Isa. 45: 2. ☆

Some were fools, they took to rebellious ways, 17
    and for their transgression they suffered punishment.
They sickened at the sight of food 18
    and drew near to the very gates of death.
So they cried to the LORD in their trouble, 19
    and he saved them from their distress;
he sent his word to heal them 20
    and bring them alive out of the pit of death.[a]
Let them thank the LORD for his enduring love 21
    and for the marvellous things he has done for men.

[a] alive ... death: *prob. rdg.; Heb.* from their corruption.

22 Let them offer sacrifices of thanksgiving
     and recite his deeds with shouts of joy.

✵ 17–22. *The deliverance of sick persons.* It is not absolutely certain that sick persons are alluded to here, and unless we follow, e.g. the Revised Standard Version, and emend *fools* to 'sick' there is no explicit Hebrew word denoting sickness in the passage ('They sickened' in verse 18 is figurative). Although deliverance from sickness is a likely interpretation of these verses, the reference could be to more general punishment of folly (see Prov. 1: 7), or, more strongly, to nearness to the realm of death caused by sin and rebellion.

18. *drew near . . . death:* death is pictured as a city whose power is already beginning to affect the afflicted person.

20. *he sent his word:* this can be understood at several levels. At the simplest level, it is a word of encouragement or hope, or a stern word which turns the fool from his folly. Next, the bringer of the word may be linked with the idea in the phrase *he sent*, so that word and messenger go closely together. Finally, the word may be personified as a divine messenger. In later Judaism, *word* can be a periphrasis for God himself, and cp. also John 1. ✵

23 Others there are who go to sea in ships
     and make their living on the wide waters.
24 These men have seen the acts of the LORD
     and his marvellous doings in the deep.
25 At his command the storm-wind rose
     and lifted the waves high.
26 Carried up to heaven, plunged down to the depths,
     tossed to and fro in peril,
27 they reeled and staggered like drunken men,
     and their seamanship was all in vain.
28 So they cried to the LORD in their trouble,

and he brought them out of their distress.
The storm sank to a murmur   29
    and the waves of the sea were stilled.
They were glad then that all was calm,   30
    as he guided them to the harbour they desired.
Let them thank the LORD for his enduring love   31
    and for the marvellous things he has done for men.
Let them exalt him in the assembly of the people   32
    and praise him in the council of the elders.

✻ 23-32. The deliverance of seafarers. The power of these verses will be apparent to anyone who has endured a rough sea crossing, even in a large stabilized ship! The section affirms the complete control of God over the sea. God it is who commands the storm-wind (verse 25) and who consequently swiftly reduces its turmoil to a murmur (verse 29). Cp. Ps. 89: 9 and note the implicit references to these verses in the New Testament account of the stilling of the storm; Matt. 8: 26. ✻

He turns rivers into desert   33
    and springs of water into thirsty ground;
he turns fruitful land into salt waste,   34
    because the men who dwell there are so wicked.
Desert he changes into standing pools,   35
    and parched land into springs of water.
There he gives the hungry a home,   36
    and they build themselves a city to live in;
they sow fields and plant vineyards   37
    and reap a fruitful harvest.
He blesses them and their numbers increase,   38
    and he does not let their herds lose strength.

39 Tyrants[a] lose their strength and are brought low
　　　in the grip of misfortune and sorrow;
40 he brings princes into contempt
　　　and leaves them wandering in a trackless waste.
41 But the poor man he lifts clear of his troubles
　　　and makes families increase like flocks of sheep.
42 The upright see it and are glad,
　　　while evildoers are filled with disgust.
43 Let the wise man lay these things to heart,
　　　and ponder the record of the LORD's enduring love.

✵ 33-43. *Conclusion: God reverses the state of things.* One of the problems of this psalm is that of its tenses. In verses 4-32, the N.E.B. prefers past tenses in English, whereas the Authorized Version has present tenses. In verses 33-43, the N.E.B. changes to present tenses, while some commentators argue for past tenses.

33. *turns rivers into desert:* cp. Isa. 50: 2.

34. *fruitful land . . . waste:* cp. the incident of Sodom and Gomorrah, Gen. 19.

35. *Desert . . . standing pools:* cp. Isa. 41: 18.

36-43. This section does not primarily assert that God regards the righteous and punishes the wicked, though it does say that the upright will be glad and evildoers will be *filled with disgust* at God's deeds (verse 42). Rather, the section speaks principally about God's gracious response to human need (verses 36-8, 41), something which in every age is difficult for those who are hard-hearted to accept. No doubt it is possible to cite examples of seafarers who are not delivered, prisoners who are not released, and poor who are not succoured, and perhaps the psalmist could have brought his own examples. But the psalmist prefers to fasten his attention on the bright side; not so that he lives in a fool's paradise, but that *the wise*

[a] Prob. rdg.; Heb. om.

man may *lay these things to heart* (verse 43), pondering *the record of the* LORD's *enduring love*, and founding his life upon that love in a world where misfortune is a hard reality from which he may not be exempt. ✣

WITH GOD'S HELP WE SHALL DO VALIANTLY

108

My heart is steadfast, O God,   1[a]
    my heart is steadfast.[b]
I will sing and raise a psalm;
    awake,[c] my spirit,
awake, lute and harp,   2
    I will awake at dawn of day.[d]
I will confess thee, O LORD, among the peoples,   3
    among the nations I will raise a psalm to thee;
for thy unfailing love is wider than the heavens   4
    and thy truth reaches to the skies.

Show thyself, O God, high above the heavens;   5
    let thy glory shine over all the earth.
Deliver those that are dear to thee;   6[e]
save with thy right hand and answer.

God has spoken from his sanctuary:[f]   7
    'I will go up now and measure out Shechem;
I will divide the valley of Succoth into plots;
Gilead and Manasseh are mine;   8

[a] *Verses 1–5: cp. Ps. 57: 7–11.*
[b] my heart is steadfast: *so some MSS.; others om.*
[c] awake: *prob. rdg.; Heb. also.*
[d] at dawn of day: *or the dawn.*
[e] *Verses 6–13: cp. Ps. 60: 5–12.*
[f] from his sanctuary: *or in his holiness.*

Ephraim is my helmet,[a] Judah my sceptre;
9 Moab is my wash-bowl, I fling my shoes at Edom;
Philistia is the target of my anger.'

10 Who can bring me to the impregnable city,
who can guide[b] me to Edom,
11 since thou, O God, hast abandoned us
and goest not forth[c] with our armies?
12 Grant us help against the enemy,
for deliverance by man is a vain hope.
13 With God's help we shall do valiantly,
and God himself will tread our enemies under foot.

✻ This psalm is composite: verses 1–5 are taken from 57: 7–11 and verses 6–13 from 60: 5–12. It is usually held that Ps. 108 is later than the other two psalms. Like Ps. 60 it is intended for use in time of military crisis, but the effect of prefacing it with 57: 7–11 instead of 60: 1–4 is to change its note of severe distress into one of confidence, doubtless more in keeping with the occasions for which it would be required. In its original context, 57: 7–11 is the conclusion of a prayer for help suitable for use in a night vigil, and though the language can be given a completely metaphorical interpretation, it is possible that a vigil setting is also presupposed in Ps. 108, and in such a setting 57: 7–11 would certainly be more appropriate than 60: 1–4. The king or commander of the army could then be imagined dedicating his cause to God in the words of this psalm just before first light on the day of a military expedition or of battle. To maintain this interpretation the translation of verse 2 will have to be more faithful to the original Hebrew than the N.E.B.'s paraphrase (see below).

It is of considerable interest to find a passage like 60: 5–12

[a] my helmet: *lit.* the refuge of my head.
[b] *So Sept.; Heb.* has guided.   [c] *So some MSS.; others add* O God.

applied to more than one set of circumstances, for this would seem to indicate that, whatever the original setting of a particular psalm (in this instance see on Ps. 60), geographical and historical data could be used with representative significance (cp. on 42: 6).

1–6. With a powerful declaration of confidence the psalmist calls on God to intervene.

1. *My heart is steadfast:* the approaching dawn, bringing light and warmth to earth, is an apt symbol of God's presence strengthening the heart of man. *my spirit:* literally 'my glory', the God-given faculty of praise (see on 30: 12).

2. Offerings of praise and thanksgiving were frequently accompanied by stringed instruments such as the *lute and harp* (cp. 150: 3). The correct translation of the second line is 'I will awake the dawn' (cp. the N.E.B. footnote) and its background is mythological. Dawn was sometimes conceived as a winged goddess (139: 9 – for these references see the Revised Standard Version or the Authorized Version; the N.E.B. generally removes the anthropomorphisms) with a womb (110: 3) and beautiful eyelids (Job 3: 9), the mother of the Day Star, Venus (Isa. 14: 12). In Greek myth she spent her nights asleep in the ocean bed and had to be wakened by another goddess. But in the present setting the personification is no more than poetic.

3. *among the peoples, among the nations:* in his overflow of confidence he wishes the whole world could hear the praises of his God.

4. *thy unfailing love . . . thy truth:* seen in God's faithfulness to his promise to protect and bless his covenant people. Herein lies the whole basis of the psalmist's confidence, as re-emphasized in the oracle that follows (verses 7–9) and his concluding prayer (verses 12f.).

5. Most appropriately God's glory at his appearing is likened to the brilliance of the rising sun.

6. In the present distress it may seem that God has abandoned his people (verse 11), but they remain *dear* to him (literally 'thy beloved'; cp. Isa. 5: 1) and it is with the knowledge of his

abiding love that this prayer is offered (cp. verse 4). This verse begins the excerpt from Ps. 60, but it links well with the theme of verses 1–5.

7–9. Confidence is strengthened by recalling an oracle promising Israel possession of Canaan and supremacy over her neighbours.

7. The oracle may derive from the sacred traditions of the sanctuary and may have been rehearsed periodically at festivals, but it could equally be a poetic recasting of the ancient promise that Israel would occupy the land. The alternative translation, 'in his holiness' (N.E.B. footnote), implies the utter dependability of his word (cp. 89: 35). Succoth and Shechem, on either side of the Jordan, were the first places where Jacob halted and settled on his return to Canaan (Gen. 33: 17f.). Hence they represent the whole land, both east and west, promised as an inheritance to his descendants.

8. *Gilead* and *Manasseh* stand for Israel's holdings in Transjordan, *Ephraim* and *Judah* for the western territory. God is here likened to a mighty warrior. Ephraim, as the most powerful tribe, is his *helmet*; Judah, with its strong tradition of Davidic kingship, is his *sceptre* (cp. Gen. 49: 10).

9. The neighbouring nations are allotted menial status, but they are not discarded as useless, for they too must serve God. The picture is of the warrior returning home, calling for his *wash-bowl*, flinging his *shoes* into a corner and shouting at his slave. *my anger:* an interpretative paraphrase, not represented in the Hebrew.

10–13. The final plea for help is also a confession that a humbling lesson has been learned. The people have been brought to see that no-one but God can *help against the enemy*. Without him they lost their battles and without him they know they can obtain no *deliverance*. But now they have learned to trust God again, there is every reason for confidence, for he remains the warrior-king who has promised to lead them to victory over their enemies.

10. *the impregnable city:* the inaccessibility of some Edomite

cities, e.g. Petra, is well known (cp. Obad. 3). The fact that this verse is no longer in the original context of Ps. 60 suggests that Edom is here a symbol of any aggressor.

11. *goest not forth . . .:* cp. 44: 9. If victory is a consequence of 'God's help' (verse 13), then the present situation of military distress suggests that he has withdrawn it.

12. *deliverance by man is a vain hope:* see on 44: 3.

13. *tread our enemies under foot:* like a goring ox (cp. 44: 5). *

MAY THE LORD REQUITE MY ACCUSERS!

109

* On the face of it, Ps. 109 contains sentiments which not only display Old Testament religion at its worst, but which ought to be abhorrent to any vaguely enlightened person. Verses 8–20 (in the N.E.B. rendering) are violent imprecations against the psalmist's false accusers and their descendants, and are incompatible with the New Testament injunction 'Love your enemies and pray for your persecutors' (Matt. 5: 44). A serious attempt to 'soften' the imprecatory character of the psalm has been made by taking verses 6–19 as the utterance of the psalmist's accusers against *him,* but this has not convinced the majority of interpreters, and in any case, in verse 20 the psalmist hopes that God will do to his enemies what has previously been wished.

In the present commentary, a mediating position will be taken. Verses 6–19 are the words of the psalmist against his enemies, but they are occasioned by the false accusations brought by the enemies. The Old Testament law of evidence required that those found guilty of giving false evidence should suffer the same penalty that the accused would have suffered had he been found guilty (Deut. 19: 16–21). The case of Naboth (1 Kings 21) shows how a man falsely accused, found guilty and executed, could have his property confiscated, presumably with disastrous results for his family. Verses 9–11 of this psalm could describe the financial plight of the family of an executed man, and verses 12f. the social rejection that would follow. Our psalmist, then, may be reflecting upon the fate that awaits him and his family if the false accusations of his enemies are accepted in court. He appeals to God that his accusers may be 'clothed with dishonour' (verse 29) and in verses 6–19, in accordance with the law of evidence, wishes upon his accusers what they are wishing upon him. Such an interpretation does not make the psalmist's imprecations any less violent, but it makes them intelligible, especially when the psalmist had tried to be good and loving to his enemies (verse 5). The psalmist is, after all, human.

However, we must not forget that the denunciation of God's wrath upon sinners is a recurring feature of the Old Testament (cp. Deut. 27: 14–26) and that within the terms of the covenant established by God's grace (Deut. 7: 7f.) was the warning 'those who defy him and show their hatred for him he repays with destruction: he will not be slow to requite any who so hate him' (Deut. 7: 10). The imprecatory parts of the psalms may be seen as a human expression of hatred against those who defy God. As they stand, they are probably not suitable for use in public worship; but it may be appropriate at penitential times of the church's year for worshippers to be reminded of God's hatred of evil, and this was done, for example, in the Commination service in the Book of Common Prayer. ✱

1 O God of my praise, be silent no longer,
2 for wicked men heap calumnies upon me.
  They have lied to my face
3 and ringed me round with words of hate.
  They have attacked me without a cause[a]
4 and accused me though I have done nothing
    unseemly.[b]

[a] *Prob. rdg.; Heb. adds* in return for my love.
[b] though . . . unseemly: *prob. rdg.; Heb. obscure.*

They have repaid me evil for good 5
    and hatred in return for my love.

They say, 'Put up some rascal to denounce him, 6
    an accuser to stand at his right side.'

But when judgement is given, that rascal will be exposed 7
    and his follies accounted a sin.

May his days be few; 8
    may his hoarded wealth[a] fall to another!

May his children be fatherless, 9
    his wife a widow!

May his children be vagabonds and beggars, 10
    driven from their homes!

May the money-lender distrain on all his goods 11
    and strangers seize his earnings!

May none remain loyal to him, 12
    and none have mercy on his fatherless children!

May his line be doomed to extinction, 13
    may their name be wiped out within a generation!

May the sins of his forefathers be remembered[b] 14
    and his mother's wickedness never be wiped out!

May they remain on record before the LORD, 15
    but may he extinguish their name from the earth!

For that man never set himself 16
    to be loyal to his friend
but persecuted the downtrodden and the poor
    and hounded the broken-hearted to their death.

Curses he loved: may the curse fall on him! 17
He took no pleasure in blessing: may no blessing be his!
He clothed himself in cursing like a garment: 18

[a] hoarded wealth: *or* charge, *cp. Acts 1: 20.*
[b] *So Pesh.; Heb. adds* before the LORD.

may it seep into his body like water
and into his bones like oil!

19 May it wrap him round like the clothes he puts on,
like the belt which he wears every day!

20 May the LORD so requite my accusers
and those who speak evil against me!

⁕ 1. *O God of my praise:* i.e. God, whom I have praised.

3. N.E.B. omits 'in return for my love' because it occurs in verse 5. The poetic division of these opening verses is problematical.

4. *accused me:* the Hebrew word is that from which the name 'Satan' is derived. In the book of Job, the Satan makes unworthy accusations against Job. *I have done nothing unseemly:* Hebrew 'I, a prayer', possibly meaning 'I (was or made) prayer (for them)'. The Hebrew for N.E.B. 'unseemly' is identical in consonants with the word for 'prayer'. The N.E.B. does not alter the fundamental sense.

6. Many commentators assume that the psalmist's imprecations begin here. N.E.B. supplies *They say*, making verse 6 the words of the accusers, verse 7 a statement by the psalmist, and verse 8 the beginning of the imprecations. This arrangement at least makes sense of the otherwise difficult 'appoint a wicked man over him' (N.E.B. '*Put up some rascal . . .*'), and is not inconsistent with the view of the psalm taken above.

7. *his follies:* Hebrew 'his prayer' – a small alteration of the Hebrew. If we retain 'prayer', and refer the verse to the false accuser whose guilt has been exposed, 'his prayer' may be his continued request for his accusations to be believed; but it is doubtful whether the Hebrew word will bear this meaning.

8–19. The imprecations.

8. *his hoarded wealth:* or 'his official position'; cp. Acts 1: 20.

10. *be vagabonds:* the N.E.B. perhaps does not bring out fully the intensity of the Hebrew expression, which wishes to see the children continually on the move. *driven from their*

homes: Hebrew 'seek from their ruined (homes'). The N.E.B. is an attempt to get good sense by offering a different interpretation of the Hebrew words, with reference to similar words in Arabic.

11. *distrain:* i.e. resort to his goods with a view to seizure for payment. It does not necessarily mean that the man would have been in debt, but that his abandoned family would soon fall prey to money-lenders.

12. *none have mercy on ... children:* the fatherless were part of the class to be specially cared for in ancient Israel (Deut. 14: 29).

14f. While the man's family is itself wiped out, all the misdeeds of his ancestors are to be remembered, especially in God's book (and see the N.E.B. footnote, 'before the LORD'). Perhaps the man's children are to be punished for his misdeeds.

16. The psalmist turns from wishing upon his accusers what the accuser wishes upon him, and describes the character of the enemy. His disregard of *the downtrodden and the poor* shows him to have little regard for the commandments of God. He could only wish people ill, not good (verse 17).

17f. The psalmist returns to imprecation, wishing that cursing may rebound on the enemy in such a way that no part of his life shall be unaffected by the sort of curses that he has directed at others.

20. A final summary, in which the psalmist requests that the false accusers will themselves suffer what they seek to inflict upon him. *

But thou, O LORD God,   21
 deal with me as befits thy honour;
  in^a the goodness of thy unfailing love deliver me,
for I am downtrodden and poor,   22
 and my heart within me is distracted.
I fade like a passing shadow,   23

[a] *Prob. rdg., cp. Targ.; Heb.* because of.

I am shaken off like a locust.

24 My knees are weak with fasting
and my flesh wastes away, so meagre is my fare.

25 I have become the victim of their taunts;
when they see me they toss their heads.

26 Help me, O LORD my God;
save me, by thy unfailing love,

27 that men may know this is thy doing
and thou alone, O LORD, hast done it.

28 They may curse, but thou dost bless;
may my opponents be put to shame,[a]
but may thy servant rejoice!

29 May my accusers be clothed with dishonour,
wrapped in their shame as in a cloak!

30 I will lift up my voice to extol the LORD,
and before a great company I will praise him.

31 For he stands at the poor man's right side
to save him from his adversaries.[b]

✱ 21–31. Petition and lamentation.

21–5. The psalmist shows that he has been affected by the
accusations. He has become *downtrodden and poor*, and his
enemies, seeing his distress, have sneered triumphantly at him.
weak with fasting: either, in his anxiety he can eat no food, or he
backs his appeal to God with abstinence from food.

26–30. He appeals to God to save him in such a way that it
will be public knowledge that God is the vindicator, and that
public witness to God's protection of the weak can be made.

31. The psalm ends with a positive declaration that God's
character is such that he stands *at the . . . right side* of the person

[a] may my . . . shame: *so Sept.; Heb.* they rose up and were put to
shame.
[b] *Prob. rdg.; Heb.* his judges.

in need, to protect him. The N.E.B. alters 'judges' to *adver-saries*, but the Hebrew may well be correct here; i.e. 'to save him from those who judge his life' implies that the psalmist fears not only false witnesses, but also false judges (cp. 1 Kings 21). ✳

YOU ARE A PRIEST FOR EVER

110

The LORD said to my lord,   1
  'You shall sit[a] at my right hand
when[b] I make your enemies the footstool under your
      feet.'
When the LORD from Zion hands you the sceptre, the   2
      symbol of your power,
  march forth through the ranks of[c] your enemies.
At birth[d] you were endowed with princely gifts   3
  and[e] resplendent[f] in holiness.
You have shone with the dew of youth since your
      mother bore you.
The LORD has sworn and will not change his purpose: 4
  'You are a priest for ever,
  in the succession of Melchizedek.'
The Lord at your right hand   5
has broken kings in the day of his anger.

[a] You shall sit: *or* Sit.
[b] *Or* until *or* while.
[c] *Or* reign in the midst of.
[d] At birth: *or* On the day of your power.
[e] you were . . . and: *or* your people offered themselves willingly; *mng. of Heb. uncertain.*
[f] *Or* apparelled.

6 So the king in his majesty,[a] sovereign of a mighty land,
       will punish nations;[b]
7   he will drink from the torrent beside the path
     and therefore will hold his head high.

* The N.E.B. footnotes indicate that this psalm contains
many problems of translation and interpretation. Modern
commentators are agreed that the psalm is ancient, and that it
is to be connected with a coronation. It is doubtful whether
references to the complete ritual for the coronation of an
ancient Near Eastern king can be detected in the text. More
probably the following promises are made to David himself,
or to a Davidic king: (a) his kingship is bestowed by God
(verses 1, 2a), (b) this kingship puts the king in a special
relationship with God (verse 3 – see below), (c) the king is
declared to be a priest (verse 4), (d) with God's help, all
enemies will be subdued (verses 1c, 2b, 5f.). A variation on this
position is that in verse 4, not the king, but Zadok (who is held
to be the high priest of Jerusalem at the time of David's
capture of the city) is addressed (see the commentary). If,
however, the reference is to the king in verse 4, then a fifth
point (e) can be made, that the psalm gives divine approval to
the assumption by the Davidic king of the rights and privileges
of the rulers of Jerusalem before the Davidic conquest, who
combined the offices of king and high priest.

In Christian interpretation the psalm has been regarded as
Messianic, particularly because of its frequent citation in the
New Testament (e.g. Heb. 1: 13). Although it is clear that the
psalm was originally addressed to a specific historical situation,
it is easy to understand how its articulation of the kingship of
God and the reign of the chosen king should have led Christian

[a] So . . . majesty: *poss. rdg.; Heb.* full of corpses, he crushed.
[b] So . . . nations: *or* He shall punish the nations – heaps of corpses,
broken heads – over a wide expanse.

interpreters to seek a complete fulfilment in a later one who should come.

1. *The LORD said:* the speaker is a priest or other cultic official who addresses the king as *my lord*. No English rendering can adequately express the Hebrew 'utterance of the LORD to my lord'. *You shall sit . . . when:* the N.E.B. here, and in verse *2a*, seems to take the words as future promises to the king. The traditional rendering 'Sit . . . until' is not easy. Whether the translation 'when' or 'until' is adopted, it is clear that at present, the subjection of enemies is incomplete and continuing; but it is God's work, and he it is who invites the king to his *right hand*. This last phrase may be completely metaphorical, or the king may actually have taken his seat on a throne in a part of the temple that was regarded symbolically as at God's right hand.

2. The N.E.B.'s extended paraphrase does not make it clear whether the *LORD from Zion* will hand *the sceptre*, or the *LORD* will hand *the sceptre* from Zion, and neither alternative is exactly clear. The phrase most likely refers to the investiture of the king with the sceptre the symbol of his rule, though the N.E.B. puts the act in the future.

3. The N.E.B. footnote gives the main possible alternative renderings. The N.E.B. text is best taken as referring to the coronation of the king, which could either be described as 'the day of your power' (N.E.B. footnote) or the day of *birth* (Ps. 2: 7). In this case, 'apparelled in holiness' (holy garments) would be a fitting parallel to the endowment of *princely gifts*. However, it is possible that the psalmist refers to a remarkable birth of the king which presaged his reign. *You have shone:* of a highly difficult, and much discussed, phrase, this much can be said for certain, that it refers to birth and dew, and that the vitality of the king (expressed by *dew*), and his designation for office since his birth, are implied.

4. *The LORD has sworn:* a strong case can be made for supposing that priest kings in Jerusalem before David's conquest often bore a name compounded with *zedek* ('righteousness')

(Gen. 14: 18; Josh. 10: 1). Thus the Davidic king is here declared to assume the ancient priestly rights and privileges of kings of Jerusalem, by being designated *a priest . . . in the succession of Melchizedek*. It is still disputed among scholars whether Davidic kings were in fact priests, but if they were, it is clear that their priesthood was to be distinguished from the Aaronic priesthood (see 2 Chron. 26: 16). The view of some interpreters that not the king, but Zadok, the Jerusalem priest at the time of David's conquest, is here addressed and accepted into the religion of Israel, explains the fact that elsewhere, Zadok seems to have been given a false genealogy (cp. 2 Sam. 8: 17 with 1 Chron. 6: 8–10 and the commentary on Chronicles in this series). In later interpretations of the psalm, the fact that Melchizedek in Gen. 14: 18 is introduced without genealogy gave rise to Messianic speculation centred upon him. The writer of the Letter to the Hebrews was able to use the present verse in order to interpret the work of Christ in priestly terms.

5. Who is addressed here? Possibly God, because *The Lord at your right hand* would be the king (verse 1) and because elsewhere in the psalm, God is addressed as 'the LORD'. However, most interpreters hold that the king is addressed, and that God is the one who has *broken kings in the day of his anger*. In this case, we must understand *at your right hand* as at Ps. 121: 5, 'The LORD is your guardian, your defence at your right hand' (strictly speaking, God is at the left hand of the king!).

6. See the N.E.B. footnote for possible alternatives. The general sense is that, empowered by God, the king will triumph in battle; not, however, for the sake of conquest but for the sake of God's justice.

7. Older commentators saw here the king refreshing himself during the battle. Newer interpreters compare 1 Kings 1: 38, where Solomon was crowned at the spring Gihon. Perhaps the coronation included the drinking of waters that were believed to be part of the divine river that flowed beneath the city of God (cp. Ps. 46: 4; Ezek. 47). *hold his head high:* be victorious. ✣

WITH ALL MY HEART WILL I PRAISE THE LORD

111

O praise the LORD.   1

With all my heart will I praise the LORD
in the company of good men, in the whole congregation.
Great are the doings of the LORD;   2
   all men study them for their delight.
His acts are full of majesty and splendour;   3
   righteousness is his for ever.
He has won a name by his marvellous deeds;   4
   the LORD is gracious and compassionate.
He gives food to those who fear him,   5
   he keeps his covenant always in mind.
He showed his people what his strength could do,   6
   bestowing on them the lands of other nations.
His works are truth and justice;   7
   his precepts all stand on firm foundations,
strongly based to endure for ever,   8
   their fabric goodness and truth.
He sent and redeemed his people;   9
he decreed that his covenant should always endure.
   Holy is his name, inspiring awe.
The fear of the LORD is the beginning[a] of wisdom,   10
and they who live by it[b] grow in understanding.
   Praise will be his for ever.

✶ Pss. 111 and 112 are acrostic psalms, in which each line of
the poem, as set out in the N.E.B., begins with a new letter of
the Hebrew alphabet (see p. 10). The first psalm is a hymn of

[a] *Or* chief part.   [b] *So Sept.; Heb.* them.

praise to God, and the second is a description of the god-fearing man. Because of the acrostic structure, both psalms consist of a series of statements, most of which can be paralleled elsewhere. There is no development of thought. The psalms were probably composed after the exile, and it is difficult to know whether they were intended for any particular cultic occasion.

1. *O praise the LORD:* see on Ps. 106: 1. The psalmist begins by declaring the importance of communal worship, as he praises God with his whole being. *good men . . . whole congregation:* these phrases are probably in apposition.

2–9. The mighty works of God.

2. *doings of the LORD:* this may mean God's great acts in history, such as the deliverance of Israel; but it can also include his creative acts in the natural world. *all men:* the Hebrew may also mean that to those who take the trouble to study them, the *doings of the LORD* are a source of delight.

3. *righteousness is his:* Hebrew 'his righteousness stands for ever'; cp. Ps. 103: 6.

5. *He gives food:* or, 'he gave food', a reference to the wilderness wanderings (Exod. 16).

6. A reference to the settlement in Canaan.

7f. *his precepts:* see Ps. 119: 4. The psalmist appears to speak of God's commandments given to man for his life in the world. These are precepts that will *endure for ever*, because they are grounded in *goodness and truth* and are the gift of the creator to his creatures.

9. The exodus and subsequent redemptions are probably meant, which were visible manifestations that God *decreed that his covenant should always endure. Holy is his name: name* means the character of God, which among other things is pure and awe-inspiring (Isa. 6: 3).

10. *fear:* this means reverent and trusting awe, and probably also includes love. See Prov. 1: 7. The N.E.B. translation of 10*b* is a paraphrase, but a very successful one. *

HAPPY IS THE MAN WHO FEARS THE LORD

112

O praise the LORD.   1

Happy is the man who fears the LORD
   and finds great joy in his commandments.
His descendants shall be the mightiest in the land,   2
   a blessed generation of good men.
His house shall be full of wealth and riches;   3
   righteousness shall be his for ever.
He is gracious, compassionate, good,   4
   a beacon in darkness for honest men.
It is right for a man to be gracious in his lending,   5
   to order his affairs with judgement.
Nothing shall ever shake him;   6
   his goodness shall be remembered for all time.
Bad news shall have no terrors for him,   7
   because his heart is steadfast, trusting in the LORD.
His confidence is strongly based, he will have no fear;   8
   and in the end he will gloat over his enemies.
He gives freely to the poor;   9
   righteousness shall be his for ever;
   in honour he carries his head high.
The wicked man shall see it with rising anger   10
   and grind his teeth in despair;
   the hopes of wicked men shall come to nothing.

✶ Ps. 112 begins where the previous psalm ends, and may be
regarded as an elaboration of 111: 10 ('The fear of the LORD is
the beginning of wisdom, and they who live by it grow in
understanding'). The introduction to Ps. 111 covers both Pss.
111 and 112.

1. *O praise the LORD:* see on Ps. 106: 1. *Happy is the man:* see Pss. 1: 1 and 119: 1. *finds great joy:* the same basic Hebrew word as for 'delight' in Ps. 111: 2. There, the contemplation of God's works gives delight; here, joy comes from the observance of God's commandments.

2. The assertion that the god-fearing man will have many and mighty descendants needs to be set alongside the many passages in the psalms where the god-fearing man is oppressed, and suffers at the hand of his enemies. Verse 7 makes it clear that the upright man will experience his share of misfortune.

3. *righteousness:* the phrase used of God in Ps. 111: 3 is applied *verbatim* to the god-fearing man here, and in verse 9. *righteousness* perhaps has a different sense when applied to man, referring to his character and his reward from God.

4. The N.E.B. transposes the lines, for the sake of clarity.

5. *judgement:* this word is ambiguous, as is the Hebrew. The verse means either that the man orders his affairs with discretion (so the Authorized Version) or that he avoids corruption and illegality in all that he does.

6. *his goodness:* the Hebrew may allude to Ps. 111: 4. God has 'won a name' (Hebrew 'memorial') 'by his marvellous deeds'; the man's *goodness shall be* ever *remembered.*

7f. *Bad news:* see verse 2. The god-fearer will not be exempted from misfortune, but his trust in God, and his belief in ultimate justification (verse 8) will sustain him.

9f. *shall see it:* i.e. the prosperity of the god-fearer, but including his acts of generosity (verses 4f., 9). The wicked will not be able to understand either the reason for the righteous man's genuine self-giving to others, or why he is rewarded by God. *

HE SETS HIS THRONE SO HIGH BUT DEIGNS TO
LOOK DOWN SO LOW

113

O praise the LORD.　　　　　　　　　　　　　　1

Praise the LORD, you that are his servants,
　　praise the name of the LORD.
Blessed be the name of the LORD　　　　　　2
　　now and evermore.
From the rising of the sun to its setting　　　3
　　may the LORD's name be praised.
High is the LORD above all nations,　　　　　4
　　his glory above the heavens.
There is none like the LORD our God　　　　5–6
　　in heaven or on earth,
who sets his throne so high
　　but deigns to look down so low;
who lifts the weak out of the dust　　　　　7
　　and raises the poor from the dunghill,
giving them a place among princes,　　　　　8
　　among the princes of his people;
who makes the woman in a childless house　9
　　a happy mother of children.[a]

✢ In this psalm the exalted majesty of God and his intimate
concern for the weak and humble are beautifully combined.
(For other examples see 1 Sam. 2: 1–10; Luke 1: 46–55). The
psalm thereby brings together two major themes of the Old
Testament, and in so doing, suggests that the psalmist himself
has a simple, but deep, personal faith in the God whom he
praises. The original setting of the psalm is unknown. 'his

[a] O praise the LORD *transposed to the beginning of Ps. 114.*

servants' (verse 1) have been identified with choirs of priests or
Levites. In later Jewish liturgical practice, the psalm was used
with others (114–18) at great festivals, especially Passover,
and may have been sung at the Last Supper (Mark 14: 26), if
this was a Passover meal.

1. *O praise the LORD:* see on Ps. 106: 1. *his servants:*
Israelite worshippers, or possibly choirs of priests or Levites.

2f. The repetition of the name of God refers to his essential
being (cp. Exod. 3: 14) and to the expression of his character
(Exod. 33: 18f.; 34: 5–7).

4. *his glory:* see Ps. 19: 1. Though the heavens declare the
might and power of the creator, yet the divine attributes are
still prior to, and above, the created order.

5f. The N.E.B. has transposed the Hebrew for the sake of
clarity. The sense is 'There is none like the LORD our God who
sets his throne so high as the heavens, but deigns to look down
so low on earth.' This expression of God's immanence and
transcendence is hardly equalled in the Old Testament, and
not surpassed.

7–9. Cp. Ps. 107: 37–43. God's concern for his creation is
best illustrated in his defence of those most needy. Even though
verse 9 may affirm that God can do what man deems to be
impossible, there is also the sense that God's care extends even
to meet the desire of an unhappy and perhaps despised woman
that she should bear children. The N.E.B., with several of the
ancient versions, transfers the closing words of the psalm to
Ps. 114. This may be correct, but it is not certainly so. ✳

WHEN ISRAEL CAME OUT OF EGYPT

114

1   O praise the LORD.*a*

When Israel came out of Egypt,
    Jacob from a people of outlandish speech,

[a] *See note on Ps. 113: 9.*

Judah became his sanctuary,   2
  Israel his dominion.
The sea looked and ran away;   3
  Jordan turned back.
The mountains skipped like rams,   4
  the hills like young sheep.
What was it, sea? Why did you run?   5
  Jordan, why did you turn back?
Why, mountains, did you skip like rams,   6
  and you, hills, like young sheep?
Dance, O earth, at the presence of the Lord,   7
  at the presence of the God of Jacob,
who turned the rock into a pool of water,   8
  the granite cliff into a fountain.

* This short psalm brings together in a few verses the exodus
from Egypt (verse 1), the wilderness wanderings (verse 8),
possibly the Sinai revelation (verse 4), the crossing of the
Jordan (verse 3*b*) and possibly the conquest of Canaan (verse 2).
The psalm does not present these events in an historical order,
but interweaves them in a beautiful poetic form. We have a
psalm of praise to God, the Lord of nature, whose lordship has
been demonstrated in saving acts on behalf of Israel.

It is impossible to determine the date and original purpose of
the psalm. Depending on the interpretation of verse 2, it could
have been composed before or after the exile. It might have
been composed prior to the return from the Babylonian exile,
which was understood as a second exodus. Because of its
content, it was a natural choice for use in the Passover service
in later Judaism.

1. *O praise the LORD:* see on Pss. 106: 1 and 113: 9. An
argument in favour of its transference to Ps. 114 is that it
provides an antecedent for 'his' in verse 2. *Israel . . . Jacob:*
clearly, here, the people descended from the patriarch Jacob.

Possibly, 'Israel' has a different sense in verse 2. *outlandish:* foreign-sounding, unfamiliar. Language, in the ancient as in the modern world, was a cultural barrier.

2. Commentators are divided on whether *Judah* and *Israel* together denote the people, as in verse 1, or whether they mean separate kingdoms of Judah and Israel after the death of Solomon, in which case *his sanctuary* may refer to Jerusalem in Judah.

3–6. Sea, river and mountain are personified. If verse 7 is to be rendered 'tremble' rather than 'dance', then the sea, river and mountains were in terror when 'Israel came out of Egypt'. By means of rhetorical questions, these same powers of nature are reminded that the same creator is still their lord, demanding their obedience.

7. The whole earth is bidden to dance (or tremble) before the God of Jacob his chosen people, who not only sustained his people in the wilderness (Exod. 17: 6) but cares for his people still. ✴

HE IS THEIR HELPER AND THEIR SHIELD

115

1   Not to us, O Lord, not to us,
         but to thy name ascribe the glory,
         for thy true love and for thy constancy.

2   Why do the nations ask,
         'Where then is their God?'
3   Our God is in high*a* heaven;
         he does whatever pleases him.
4   Their idols are silver and gold,
         made by the hands of men.
5   They have mouths that cannot speak,
         and eyes that cannot see;

[a] high: *so Sept.; Heb. om.*

they have ears that cannot hear, 6
   nostrils, and cannot smell;
with their hands they cannot feel, 7
   with their feet they cannot walk,
   and no sound comes from their throats.
Their makers grow to be like them, 8
   and so do all who trust in them.

But Israel trusts in the LORD; 9
   he is their helper and their shield.
The house of Aaron trusts in the LORD; 10
   he is their helper and their shield.
Those who fear the LORD trust in the LORD; 11
   he is their helper and their shield.
The LORD remembers us, and he will bless us; 12
   he will bless the house of Israel,
   he will bless the house of Aaron.
The LORD will bless all who fear him, 13
   high and low alike.

May the LORD give you increase, 14
   both you and your sons.
You are blessed by the LORD, 15
   the LORD who made heaven and earth.
The heavens, they are the LORD's; 16
   the earth he has given to all mankind.
It is not the dead who praise the LORD, 17
   not those who go down into silence;
but we, the living,[a] bless the LORD, 18
   now and for evermore.

O praise the LORD.

[a] the living: *so Sept.; Heb. om.*

✻ There are two main problems of interpretation in this psalm: the situation implied in verses 1f., and whether verses 9–11 are statements or exhortations. Many commentators assume that verses 1f. are a plea for God's help at a time of national humiliation ('Why do the nations . . .?'). Israel prays for deliverance ('ascribe the glory', verse 1), but so that God and not Israel will be glorified. The phrase 'ascribe the glory' is, however, unclear, and the psalm could just as well be understood as Israel's recognition that a recent triumph (e.g. the return from exile) was God's achievement and not Israel's. Verse 2 does not necessarily imply the humiliation of Israel; the taunt of the nations could be triumphantly thrown back in their faces in view of a recent triumph. If the interpretation in terms of a prayer for deliverance is sustained, verses 9–11 would be better understood as an exhortation to Israel to trust but, in turn, this interpretation of verses 9–11 does not of itself compel acceptance of the view that the psalm is a prayer for deliverance.

While it would be best not to be dogmatic about the overall interpretation, verses 3–8 are an incomparable statement about the uniqueness of the God of Israel and the folly of idolatry, and verses 12–16 assure blessing for God's people. In some traditions, Pss. 114 and 115 are treated as one psalm.

4–8. The mockery of idols is found at Ps. 135: 15–18 in almost identical language, and at Isa. 44: 9–20; Jer. 10: 1–16.

9. *But Israel trusts:* the N.E.B. follows the Septuagint and Peshitta against the Hebrew, which is an imperative: 'O Israel, trust in the LORD.' In Ps. 135: 19f. there is a similar passage (but with the verb 'to bless') which is clearly imperative. *Israel* probably means the whole nation.

10. *The house of Aaron:* the priests descended from Aaron.

11. *Those who fear the LORD:* this may refer to non-Jews who are attracted to the worship of the God of Israel, but more probably (see verse 13), it is a term for worshippers, which includes the Israelites and the priests.

12. *The LORD remembers us:* the N.E.B. makes this verse

continue the affirmations of verses 9–11. The Hebrew can also be translated 'The LORD has remembered us, and he will bless us', indicating that the prayer for deliverance (if we so interpret verses 1f.) has been answered.

14f. These verses may be a continuation of the preceding passage – 'The LORD shall increase you . . .' The N.E.B. takes verse 14 as a wish.

16. *the earth he has given*: cp. Ps. 8: 6–8.

17f. These verses may be a plea to God not to let his people perish and go to the place of *silence* where God cannot be praised (cp. Ps. 88: 10–12); or the survivors may exult in their recent deliverance, while they reflect that the living God (verses 3, 16) is praised by those who live. *O praise the LORD*: see Ps. 106: 1. ✻

HE HAS HEARD ME AND LISTENS TO MY PRAYER

116

I love the LORD, for he has heard me	1
and listens to my prayer;	
for he has given me a hearing	2
whenever I have cried to him.	
The cords of death bound me,	3
Sheol held me in its grip.	
Anguish and torment held me fast;	
so I invoked the LORD by name,	4
'Deliver me, O LORD, I beseech thee;	
for I am thy slave.'[a]	
Gracious is the LORD and righteous,	5
our God is full of compassion.	
The LORD preserves the simple-hearted;	6
I was brought low and he saved me.	

[a] for . . . slave: *transposed from the beginning of verse 16; Heb. adds* O LORD.

7 Be at rest once more, my heart,
       for the LORD has showered gifts upon you.
8 He has^a rescued me from death
       and my feet from stumbling.^b
9 I will walk in the presence of the LORD
       in the land of the living.

10 I was sure that I should be swept away,
       and my distress was bitter.
11 In panic I cried,
       'How faithless all men are!'
12 How can I repay the LORD
       for all his gifts to me?
13 I will take in my hands the cup of salvation
       and invoke the LORD by name.
14 I will pay my vows to the LORD
       in the presence of all his people.
15 A precious thing in the LORD's sight
       is the death of those who die faithful to him.
16 ^cI am thy slave, thy slave-girl's son;
       thou hast undone the bonds that bound me.
17 To thee will I bring a thank-offering
       and invoke the LORD by name.
18 I will pay my vows to the LORD
       in the presence of all his people,
19   in the court. of the LORD's house,
       in the midst of you, Jerusalem.

       O praise the LORD.

[a] *So Sept.; Heb.* Thou hast.
[b] *So Pesh.; Heb. adds* my eyes from weeping.
[c] *Prob. rdg.; Heb. prefixes* For I am thy slave, O LORD; *see note on*
verse 4.

✻ This psalm is a hymn of thanksgiving to God, who has heard the prayer of the psalmist, and delivered him from his troubles. The nature of the troubles is not specified, but they may have been sickness (verse 3) or malicious insults (verse 11). The psalmist appears to give thanks publicly for his deliverance (verses 14, 18), offering appropriate gifts (verses 13, 17). He is confident that God will always hear his prayer (verse 2), that he will enjoy fulness of life as God's servant (verse 9) and that, at death, his departure will be 'A precious thing' to God (verse 15). A date is difficult to determine; many experts hold that the linguistic forms suggest that the psalm was composed late after the exile, although others argue that the expression 'slave-girl's son' can be a description of the king.

1. *I love the LORD . . .*: the Hebrew is awkward – literally 'I love, for the LORD hears my voice, my supplications.' The N.E.B. has made slight alterations, but brings out the main point well, that the psalmist's love for God arises from his experience of God's ready response to his prayers.

2. *whenever I have cried*: literally 'and in my days I shall cry (to him)'. The N.E.B. has again slightly altered the text. The Hebrew may mean 'in my days (of distress) I shall cry (to him)'.

3f. The distress of the psalmist (possibly sickness) was such that he felt that death already had him *in its grip*. The N.E.B. transposes *for I am thy slave* from verse 16, where the phrase occurs twice.

5f. The psalmist asserts not only his own deliverance, but that it is God's nature to deliver the *simple-hearted*, i.e. those who find it difficult to defend themselves. This readiness of God to act for the weak and needy is part of what is meant by saying that God is righteous.

7. The psalmist addresses his *heart* (Hebrew *nephesh*), i.e. his emotional and spiritual life, personified. It needs to be anxious no longer, though its anxiety continues after the deliverance.

9. *in the land of the living:* in this world, in contrast to the dead world of Sheol (verse 3).

10f. The psalmist recalls once more his troubles. *I was sure:*

the meaning of the Hebrew is uncertain. The most common meanings of the Hebrew yield a literal translation: 'I believed, because (or that) I shall speak.' The passage is to be taken either with the N.E.B., or as as meaning that in spite of his distress and panic, the psalmist kept his faith in God. *How faithless:* the contrast appears to be between God who is trustworthy and man, who cannot be relied upon.

12. *How can I repay:* the implication may be that it is impossible to thank God adequately for his gifts.

13. *the cup of salvation:* probably the cup containing the wine of thank-offering in gratitude for salvation (cp. Num. 28: 7), or a metaphor for salvation.

14. *my vows:* possibly vows made by the psalmist when he was in distress, and prayed for deliverance. These would include thank-offerings.

15. *A precious thing:* the sense may be that God does not allow those *faithful to him* to die an untimely death. However, it is clear that such people have to die sometime, and the N.E.B. implies that such deaths are especially noticed by God.

16–19. The psalmist expresses the intimate, yet distanced, nature of his relationship to God (verse 16) and re-affirms his intentions to give thanks in the Jerusalem temple. *thy slave, thy slave-girl's son:* cp. Ps. 86: 16. A servant born of a slave-girl was permanently bound to his master (Exod. 21: 4); thus the psalmist conceives his relation to God. *O praise the LORD:* see Ps. 106: 1. *

PRAISE THE LORD

117

1   Praise the LORD, all nations,
            extol him, all you peoples;
2   for his love protecting us is strong,
            the LORD's constancy is everlasting.

         O praise the LORD.

✻ The shortest psalm in the psalter has a universal perspective.
All nations and peoples are summoned to worship the God of
Israel. It is in dealings with Israel that he has uniquely displayed
his covenant loyalty and constancy (verse 2), but in these acts
his purpose for all nations has been disclosed. The psalm is
usually thought to have been composed after the exile.

2. *O praise the LORD:* see Ps. 106: 1. ✻

THE STONE WHICH THE BUILDERS REJECTED
HAS BECOME THE CHIEF CORNER-STONE

118

✻ This psalm contains many memorable phrases; verses 22f.
are quoted or alluded to in numerous New Testament
passages (e.g. Matt. 21: 42 and parallels) and verse 26 provides
the background to Jesus' entry to Jerusalem (Matt. 21: 9 and
parallels). It is, however, difficult to determine its place in Old
Testament worship and history. While verses 1–4 and probably 22–9 imply congregational praise, verses 5–21 appear to
be an individual thanksgiving for deliverance from danger.
Yet the individual was surrounded by nations (verse 10), so he
may well be Israel personified, and verses 5–21 may have been
spoken by a cultic representative of the congregation or by the
king. From verses 19f., some commentators have suggested
that the psalm was used at a procession into the temple, and
comparisons have been made with the so-called 'entrance
liturgies', Pss. 15 and 24. Those experts may be correct who
argue that the psalm is composed of several originally
separate liturgical fragments (see on verse 5). Whatever its
original setting and purpose, it established itself in Jewish
worship as part of the Hallel (Pss. 113–118) sung at great
festivals, including Passover, and in Christian worship as a
psalm for Easter. ✻

> It is good to give thanks to the LORD,   1
>   for his love endures for ever.

2 Declare it, house of*a* Israel:
  his love endures for ever.

3 Declare it, house of Aaron:
  his love endures for ever.

4 Declare it, you that fear the LORD:
  his love endures for ever.

5 When in my distress I called to the LORD,
  his answer was to set me free.

6 The LORD is on my side, I have no fear;
  what can man do to me?

7 The LORD is on my side, he is my helper,
  and I shall gloat over my enemies.

8 It is better to find refuge in the LORD
  than to trust in men.

9 It is better to find refuge in the LORD
  than to trust in princes.

10 All nations surround me,
  but in the LORD's name I will drive them away.

11 They surround me on this side and on that,
  but in the LORD's name I will drive them away.

12 They surround me like bees at the honey;*b*
  they attack me, as fire attacks brushwood,
  but in the LORD's name I will drive them away.

13 They thrust*c* hard against me so that I nearly fall;
  but the LORD has helped me.

14 The LORD is my refuge and defence,
  and he has become my deliverer.

15 Hark! Shouts of deliverance

[a] house of: *so Sept.; Heb. om.*
[b] at the honey: *so Sept.; Heb. om.*
[c] *So Sept.; Heb.* Thou dost thrust.

in the camp of the victors[a]!

With his right hand the LORD does mighty deeds,
    the right hand of the LORD raises up.[b]   16

I shall not die but live   17
    to proclaim the works of the LORD.

The LORD did indeed chasten me,   18
    but he did not surrender me to Death.

---

* 1–4. The whole nation, and groups within it are called upon to declare that the love of God *endures for ever*. *house of Israel:* probably, the whole nation. *house of Aaron:* the priests descended from Aaron. *you that fear the LORD:* this may refer to non-Jews who are attracted to the worship of the God of Israel, but more probably, it is a term for worshippers, which includes the Israelites and the priests. Cp. Ps. 115: 9–11.

5. *When in my distress:* Hebrew 'Out of the distress (or strait place) I called to Yah, Yah answered me in the broad place.' The name Yah is used several times in the psalm (at verses 14, 17, 18, 19). It is generally held to be a contracted form of Yahweh, and appears both in very early poetic passages in the Old Testament (Exod. 15: 2), and also in the phrase 'Hallelujah' (Ps. 106: 1). The fact that it occurs in this psalm only in verses 5–19 may support the view that these verses are a fragment originally separate from what precedes and follows, or a quotation from an older poem. The nature of the distress is not clear (see verses 10–13), but the Hebrew provides a contrast between the 'strait place' and the 'broad place', which latter is God's gift in deliverance.

7. *I shall gloat:* I shall look in triumph upon my (defeated) enemies.

8f. *It is better:* this may either be a religious proverb, or a reference to a recent example of failure by human allies. The

[a] *Or* righteous.
[b] *So some MSS.; others repeat* with his right hand the LORD does mighty deeds.

tenses of verse 10 are relevant. The Hebrew is strictly 'all nations surrounded me' referring to a past event. The N.E.B., however, takes verses 10–13 to be general statements, with the result that verses 8f. are more proverbial. The *princes* (verse 9) may be foreign rulers rather than nobles within the Israelite community.

10–13. *All nations surround:* the use of the present tense by the N.E.B. goes against the sense of verses 5 and 13, that the distress is now past, although it is true that we cannot identify the past distress, and that the psalm would be applicable to many situations. *in the LORD's name:* i.e. trusting in his character and promises, and confident of his help. *they attack me:* Hebrew 'they were quenched like a fire of thorn'. If this is correct, the line refers to the defeat of the enemies, and since the verse has three lines, the third line was possibly wrongly repeated from verses 10f. However, the Septuagint took the line as describing the attack by the enemies, not their defeat, and the N.E.B. makes good sense in this same direction. *They thrust:* the Hebrew 'Thou didst thrust' (the N.E.B. footnote renders the tense in accordance with its overall interpretation of these verses), if correct, would be best addressed to the enemy; but the change of person is very abrupt.

14. This verse is identical with Exod. 15: 2 (where the N.E.B. translates it slightly differently from here) and may be a quotation from the ancient hymn of triumph.

15f. The psalmist draws attention to victory shouts, and it is possible that verses 15c and 16 give the content of the cries. *camp:* this illustrates the difficulty of interpreting the psalm, since while it may refer to a battle-camp, some commentators take the Hebrew (literally 'tents') to refer to the Israelites encamped around Jerusalem for the Feast of Tabernacles. *victors* (or 'righteous' – N.E.B. footnote): those whose victory depended as much on their loyalty to God's commandments as on any fighting skill.

17f. The speaker implies that he was close to death (cp. verses 5, 13) and that part of this was God's chastening. But he

lives so that he may *proclaim the works of the LORD*, i.e. God's
acts of deliverance. Among other possibilities, the words apply
to Israel's experience of the Babylonian exile and delivery from
it. ✶

Open to me the gates of victory;*a*   19
    I will enter by them and praise the LORD.
This is the gate of the LORD;   20
    the victors*b* shall make their entry through it.
I will praise thee, for thou hast answered me   21
    and hast become my deliverer.
The stone which the builders rejected   22
    has become the chief corner-stone.
This is the LORD's doing;   23
    it is marvellous in our eyes.
This is the day on which the LORD has acted:*c*   24
    let us exult and rejoice in it.
We pray thee, O LORD, deliver us;   25
    we pray thee, O LORD, send us prosperity.
Blessed in the name of the LORD are all who come;   26
    we bless you from the house of the LORD.
The LORD is God; he has given light to us,   27
the ordered line of pilgrims*d* by the horns of the altar.
Thou art my God and I will praise thee;   28
    my God, I will exalt thee.
It is good to give thanks to the LORD,   29
    for his love endures for ever.

✶ 19–21. If the background to these verses is a triumphal
procession, then the gates of victory may be an entrance to

[a] *Or* righteousness.   [b] *Or* righteous.   [c] *Or* which the LORD has made.
[d] the . . . pilgrims: *so Scroll; Heb.* bind the pilgrimage with cords.

Jerusalem reserved for victors. Using the rendering 'gates of righteousness' (and see also the N.E.B. footnote to verse 20) some interpreters refer to Pss. 15 and 24, and suggest that would-be entrants to the temple area were questioned as to their loyalty to God. However, the speaker demands entry as of right, in virtue of his victory, unless we suppose that verse 20 is the reply of a doorkeeper qualifying the demand made in verse 19, i.e. (only) *the victors shall make their entry through it*.

22–4. With the use of a building metaphor, the worshippers declare that what to the enemies seemed a rejected person or people was to God something precious; God acted to save, and the worshippers acknowledge that the victory was his entirely. The appropriateness of the verses to many situations, including the Babylonian exile, and the death and resurrection of Jesus Christ is obvious. *chief corner-stone:* this was either an important foundation stone, or the keystone, for example, of an arch.

25–7. These verses may be part of a liturgy of blessing. The speakers ask for divine deliverance (verse 25) to which priests respond with a blessing (verse 26), followed by a reply from the original speakers (verse 27). The relation of these verses to the preceding verses is not clear, unless the returning victors are also pilgrims. *deliver us:* the Hebrew is transliterated as 'Hosanna' in the New Testament, a kind of salutation. Verse 27 is difficult. The light which God has given may be the light mentioned in the priestly blessing (Num. 6: 25), or it may more generally be deliverance, or spiritual enlightenment from God's laws and promises. Verse 27*b* is probably corrupt beyond recovery. The N.E.B. makes the speakers the pilgrims, who are standing close to the *horns of the altar*. The Hebrew is traditionally interpreted 'bind the (animal offered at the) pilgrimage with cords, until (we reach) the horns of the altar'. *horns:* these were projections at the four corners of the altar. If they were cut off, the altar was defiled (Amos 3: 14).

28f. The psalm closes with language close to that of Exod. 15: 2*c, d* (verse 28) and with a repetition of verse 1. ✻

O HOW I LOVE THY LAW!

119

✣ Psalm 119 is unique in the Psalter. It is an elaborate acrostic psalm, with the first 8 lines beginning with the first letter of the Hebrew alphabet, the next 8 with the second letter, and so on. The Hebrew alphabet has 22 letters, giving a total of 176 lines or verses. In addition, 8 main terms are used to describe the totality of God's revelation, and in some cases, each one of these 8 terms is used successively in an 8-line section (e.g. verses 57–64). Although it must be noted that one or two terms in addition to the eight occur here and there, it is clear that a determined effort has been made by the psalmist to construct the psalm according to a rigid pattern.

Although commentators are agreed that the psalm was composed late after the exile, only interesting suggestions can be made about its author and purpose. From verses such as 78, 81–8, 95, 110, 134, 150, 157, 161, it has been suggested that the psalmist was often in danger from those who disregarded God's law, and even from those in authority (verse 161). In this case, we can picture him as a faithful teacher and servant, standing out against the indifference of his day. Another view (which is not necessarily irreconcilable with the previous suggestion) is that Ps. 119 was originally composed to end the Psalter, just as Ps. 1 was written to begin it. The psalmist has tried to sum up all that has gone before in the Psalter, and references to oppression may reflect the many descriptions of oppression in the Psalter.

Ps. 119 is the greatest expression in the Old Testament of love for God's law (cp. also Ps. 19), and it represents a religious attitude that is to be found in later Judaism in Pharisaism at its best. The psalmist stands very close indeed to God. Where he uses terms to describe God's revelation, he uses them more often with the qualifying word 'thy'. Thus it is not God's law or decrees as abstract things that the psalmist is concerned

PSALM 119	Law (tōrāh)	Commandments (miṣvōth)	Precepts (piqqudīm)	Statutes (huqqīm)	Word(s) (dābār)	Promise ('imrāh)	Instruction ('ēdōth)	Decree(s) (mishpāṭ(īm))
keep, heed, obey, follow, observe	34, 44, 55 'dwell upon'	60 (run, 32) (fulfil, 166)	4, 56, 63, 69, 100, 134, 168	5, 8, 145 (resolved to fulfil, 112) (be occupied with, 117)	17, 57, 101, 'in my obedience', 9 'holding to'	67	2, 22, 88, 146, 167, 168 (hold fast to, 31)	106 (set before me, 30)
not forget	61, 109, 153	176 (not stray from, 10)	93, 141 (not forsake, 87) (do not stray, 110)	83	16		(give thought, 95)	(cherished, 52) (not swerve, 102)
meditate, study	97* (dwell upon, 55)		15, 78	23, 48		148* (treasure in my heart, 11)	99*	
hoped for fulfilment of, put hope in		(longing for, 131) (put trust in, 66)	(long for, 40)		74, 81, 114, 147 (trust in, 42)			43 (longing for, 20)
love	97, 113, 163, 165	47, [48], 127	159				119	(stand in awe of, 120)
delight in continually, find delight	70, 77,* 92,* 174*	47, 143*		16		(jubilant over, 162)	24* (found joy, 14) (joy,* 111)	(cherished, 52)

PSALM 119 (cont.)

teach	34 'give insight to obey'	(do not hide, 19)	27 'show me way', 104 'learn'	12, 26, 33, 64, 68, 124, 135, 171, 71 'school me'				108
give understanding, insight		73 'show how I may learn' (make me walk in path of, 35)	93		169	(make step firm, 133)	125 (dispose my heart toward, 36)	
give, grant life				my song, 54	17, 25, 107 (revive me), 37 (variant reading)	50, 154		149, 156
other descriptions	truth, 142	stand for ever, 86 / has no limit, 96 / true, 151 / justice itself, 172			planted firm in heaven, 89 / lamp/light, 105 / founded in truth, 160	sweeter than honey, 103 / tested through and through, 140	wonderful, 129 / ever just, 144 / given eternal foundations, 152	good, 39 / just, 75 / straight and true, 137 / everlasting, 160

1. * means that a noun related to the verbal stem is used.

2. ( ), as in '(cherished, 52)', indicates the use of a different verb to that listed in the left-hand column, but one with a similar meaning.

3. Entries in inverted commas, e.g. 71 'school me', indicate that the Hebrew verb listed in the left-hand column is used, but with a rendering not noted there.

with, but 'thy law', 'thy decrees' – things pointing him to
God.

The accompanying plan seeks to plot out the use of the
eight main terms. The N.E.B. consistently uses the same
English word for the same Hebrew word, which is a great help
to the reader. There is slightly more freedom in the rendering
of the verbs noted in the left-hand column. A consideration of
the plan reveals the following main usage of the key words.

(*a*) God's 'law' is probably something written, though not
confined to legal prescriptions. The psalmist can meditate upon
it, love it, and delight in it. Yet it contains that which is to be
obeyed, and not forgotten.

(*b*) God's 'commandments' have much in common with
his 'law', but they are not the object of meditation, and
although they are no doubt either written down or a body of
teaching known by heart, verse 19 'do not hide' suggests that
on occasion, new aspects of God's commands are disclosed to
the psalmist.

(*c*) God's 'precepts' are primarily to be observed, and not
forgotten; but they are also the object of meditation. The term
is probably very close in meaning to 'law' in this psalm,
perhaps with more emphasis on specific instructions.

(*d*) The most striking feature about 'statutes' is the psalmist's
repeated prayer that God will teach him his statutes. It is
difficult to know whether this is a request for deeper insight
into what has been enacted, or a request for new statutes.

(*e*) With God's 'word' and 'promise' we reach a different
area of meaning. The 'word' and 'promise' are certainly a
record of what God has done in the past, and what therefore
reveals his character. In addition, the psalmist expects God to
act in accordance with his words and promises. When he does,
the result will be to 'give life', probably by rescuing the
psalmist from his troubles.

(*f*) 'Instruction' seems to go closely with 'law' and
'precepts' in usage in the psalm.

(*g*) 'Decree' has two main senses: a judgement in favour of the psalmist against his adversaries, which 'gives life' to the psalmist; and past decisions to which the psalmist will be obedient.

The total picture that emerges is not of something static, but of something many-sided and dynamic. God's revelation is partly written, and is partly commandment and partly story containing promise. It is to be obeyed, loved, and understood ever more deeply. In itself it gives light and guidance; but it establishes fellowship with a living God who even now acts in accordance with his promises to deliver the psalmist, and to illuminate his understanding.

The practice that has long been the tradition in some churches, that large sections of Ps. 119 are recited in the course of daily or weekly offices, while not in any way bad in itself, should not obscure the fact that the psalm must be the object of detailed study and thought if it is to be properly appreciated. ✳

Happy are they whose life is blameless,   1
    who conform to the law of the LORD.
Happy are they who obey his instruction,   2
    who set their heart on finding him;
who have done no wrong   3
    and have lived according to his will.
Thou, Lord, hast laid down thy precepts   4
    for men to keep them faithfully.
If only I might hold a steady course,   5
    keeping thy statutes!
I shall never be put to shame   6
    if I fix my eyes on thy commandments.
I will praise thee in sincerity of heart   7
    as I learn thy just decrees.
Thy statutes will I keep faithfully;   8
    O do not leave me forsaken.

✶ 1–8. Verses '*ālep*. The psalm opens probably in a way deliberately like Ps. 1: 1. After stating in general terms the blessedness of the man who sets his whole heart to obey God's revelation, the psalmist indicates that he does not include himself among those who achieve complete success with obedience (verse 5). It is noteworthy that the final verse of the psalm (verse 176) also makes a deliberate contrast with the opening verses. The psalmist is not in any way self-righteous; he is aware of his weakness, and of his dependence upon God's grace. ✶

9 How shall a young man steer an honest course?
    By holding to thy word.
10 With all my heart I strive to find thee;
    let me not stray from thy commandments.
11 I treasure thy promise in my heart,
    for fear that I might sin against thee.
12 Blessed art thou, O LORD;
    teach me thy statutes.
13 I say them over, one by one,
    the decrees that thou hast proclaimed.
14 I have found more joy along the path of thy instruction
    than in[a] any kind of wealth.
15 I will meditate on thy precepts
    and keep thy paths ever before my eyes.
16 In thy statutes I find continual delight;
    I will not forget thy word.

✶ 9–16. Verses *bēt*. The dominant thought of this section is that of continual preoccupation with God's revelation so that it reaches the deepest levels of thought and life. The section speaks of meditation (verse 15), treasuring in the heart (verse

a] So Pesh.; Heb. *as in*.

11), continual delight (verse 16) and repetition (verse 13). On
the basis of verse 9, some have supposed the psalmist to be a
young man. *

Grant this to me, thy servant: let me live   17
   and, living, keep thy word.
Take the veil from my eyes, that I may see   18
   the marvels that spring from thy law.
I am but a stranger here on earth,[a]   19
   do not hide thy commandments from me.
My heart pines with longing   20
   day and night for thy decrees.
The proud have felt thy rebuke;   21
   cursed are those who turn from thy commandments.
Set me free from scorn and insult,   22
   for I have obeyed thy instruction.
The powers that be sit scheming together against me;   23
   but I, thy servant, will study thy statutes.
Thy instruction is my continual delight;   24
   I turn to it for counsel.

* 17–24. Verses *gīmel*. There are some possible details about
the psalmist in this section. He is described as a stranger (verse
19), that is, an Israelite living away from his home, family and
community, and he is the object of scheming by those in
authority (verse 23) as well as scorned and insulted (verse 22).
Possibly, however, verse 19 describes not his status in Israel,
but his status in the world; he is passing through the world as a
temporary guest, and as such, desires God's guidance and
protection. Verse 18 is a prayer for a deeper understanding of
the marvels written in the record of God's deeds. *

[a] *Or* in the land.

25 I lie prone in the dust;
     grant me life according to thy word.
26 I tell thee all I have done and thou dost answer me;
     teach me thy statutes.
27 Show me the way set out in thy precepts,
     and I will meditate on thy wonders.
28 I cannot rest for misery;
     renew my strength in accordance with thy word.
29 Keep falsehood far from me
     and grant me the grace of living by thy law.
30 I have chosen the path of truth
     and have set thy decrees before me.
31 I hold fast to thy instruction;
     O LORD, let me not be put to shame.
32 I will run the course set out in thy commandments,
     for they gladden my heart.

✴ 25-32. Verses *dālet*. In this section the Hebrew word *derek* = way, is prominent: verse 26, *all I have done* (literally 'my ways'), verse 27, *the way set out in thy precepts*, verse 29, *falsehood* (literally 'way of falsehood'), verse 30, *the path* (literally 'way') *of truth*, verse 32, *the course* (literally 'way') *set out in thy commandments*. Basically, the psalmist's request is that God will keep him from the false way (verse 29), and will show him the true way (verse 27), whereupon the psalmist, whose ways are known to God (verse 26) will follow God's way (verse 32). For a similar use of *derek* see Ps. 1: 6. ✴

33 Teach me, O LORD, the way set out in thy statutes,
     and in keeping them I shall find my reward.
34 Give me the insight to obey thy law
     and to keep it with all my heart;
35 make me walk in the path of thy commandments,

for that is my desire.

Dispose my heart toward thy instruction   36
  and not toward ill-gotten gains;
turn away my eyes from all that is vile,   37
  grant me life by thy word.[a]
Fulfil thy promise for thy servant,   38
  the promise made to those who fear thee.
Turn away the censure which I dread,   39
  for thy decrees are good.
How I long for thy precepts!   40
  In thy righteousness grant me life.

✶ 33–40. Verses *hē*. The fact that the letter *hē*, which begins the next eight lines marks a causative sense in Hebrew (e.g. simple sense – 'walk'; causative sense – 'make me walk'; cp. verse 35) makes this section consist mainly of requests in which the divine initiative and power in the psalmist's life are stressed: *Teach me . . ., Give me the insight . . . make me walk*. The inability of the psalmist to be true to God without God's help is thus strongly emphasized.

33. *I shall find my reward:* cp. Ps. 19: 11. The Hebrew is difficult, and is traditionally rendered 'unto the end'. *reward* is probably right; the reward is not something gained by the psalmist's unaided efforts, as this whole section makes clear.

39. *thy decrees are good:* i.e. God's sentence against those who insult the psalmist. ✶

Thy love never fails; let it light on me, O LORD,   41
  and thy deliverance, for that was thy promise;
then I shall have my answer to the man who taunts   42
    me,
  because I trust in thy word.

[a] *by thy word: so some MSS.; others* in thy ways.

43 Rob me not of my power to speak the truth,[a]
    for I put my hope in thy decrees.
44 I will heed thy law continually,
    for ever and ever;
45 I walk in freedom wherever I will,
    because I have studied thy precepts.
46 I will speak of thy instruction before kings
    and will not be ashamed;
47 in thy commandments I find continuing delight;
    I love them with all my heart.[b]
48 I will welcome thy commandments[c]
    and will meditate on thy statutes.

✻ 41–8. Verses *wāw*. The psalmist looks forward to deliverance
from his adversaries (verse 41), a deliverance which will give
freedom (verse 45), and confidence to speak of God's ways to
those who taunt him (verse 42) or even to kings (verse 46),
provided that he retains his ability to speak the truth (verse 43).

41. The N.E.B. gives a very free rendering, designed to
make clear that God's love which the psalmist prays to God to
exercise, is that love which *never fails*.

43. *Rob me not*: either, when the psalmist makes his apology
in court, or generally, with regard to testifying about God's
goodness. *thy decrees*: probably, God's sentence in favour of the
psalmist.

45. *walk in freedom*: cp. Ps. 118: 5*b*.

48. *welcome thy commandments*: literally 'lift up my hands
unto thy commandments'. Although it is a conjecture, there
are strong reasons for reading a text that would be translated
'I will lift up my hands unto thee', i.e. pray to thee. Commandments were mentioned in the previous verse, and it is

[a] So Pesh.; *Heb. adds* very much.
[b] with all my heart: *prob. rdg., cp. Sept.; Heb. om.*
[c] *Prob. rdg.; Heb. adds* which I love.

unusual for one of the main words to appear twice in one
section. If commandments were deleted from this verse, verses
41–8 would mention each of the eight main words in turn. ✳

Remember the word spoken to me, thy servant,	49
on which thou hast taught me to fix my hope.	
In time of trouble my consolation is this,	50
that thy promise has given me life.	
Proud men treat me with insolent scorn,	51
but I do not swerve from thy law.	
I have cherished thy decrees all my life long,	52
and in them I find consolation, O Lord.	
Gusts of anger seize me as I think of evil men	53
who forsake thy law.	
Thy statutes are the theme of my song[a]	54
wherever I make my home.	
In the night I remember thy name, O Lord,	55
and dwell upon thy law.	
This is true of me,	56
that I have kept thy precepts.	

✳ 49–56. Verses *zayin*. This section emphasizes the steadfast
obedience of the psalmist to God's laws, in spite of every
difficulty; he is sustained by God's promises (verses 49f.).

49. *Remember*: perhaps the need to use a verb beginning
with the appropriate Hebrew letter accounts for the plea to
remember, when it is clear elsewhere in the psalm that so much
depends on God's unsolicited help. It is, however, part of the
mystery of prayer that the man of God requests what he knows
is already being given.

52. *thy decrees* is clearly past decrees, perhaps God's judgement on Israel's enemies, recorded in the historical traditions.

[a] the theme of my song: *or* wonderful to me.

54. *wherever I make my home:* literally 'in the house of my sojournings' (see on verse 19). ✳

Thou, LORD, art all I have;[a]   57
  I have promised to keep thy word.
With all my heart I have tried to please thee;   58
  fulfil thy promise and be gracious to me.
I have thought much about the course of my life   59
  and always turned back to thy instruction;
I have never delayed but always made haste   60
  to keep thy commandments.
Bands of evil men close round me,   61
  but I do not forget thy law.
At midnight I rise to give thee thanks   62
  for the justice of thy decrees.
I keep company with all who fear thee,   63
  with all who follow thy precepts.
The earth is full of thy never-failing love;   64
  O LORD, teach me thy statutes.

✳ 57–64. Verses *ḥēt*. God's law is a protection against the trials and tribulations of life (verses 59, 61) both night and day (verse 62).

57. *all I have:* see on Ps. 16: 5a. ✳

Thou hast shown thy servant much kindness,   65
  fulfilling thy word, O LORD.
Give me insight, give me knowledge,   66
  for I put my trust in thy commandments.
I went astray before I was punished;   67
  but now I pay heed to thy promise.

[a] all I have: *lit.* my portion.

Thou art good and thou doest good; 68
   teach me thy statutes.

Proud men blacken my name with lies, 69
   yet I follow thy precepts with all my heart;

their hearts are thick and gross; 70
   but I continually delight in thy law.

How good it is for me to have been punished, 71
   to school me in thy statutes!

The law thou hast ordained means more to me 72
   than a fortune in gold and silver.

* 65–72. Verses *ṭēt*. In this section, the Hebrew word *ṭōb*, 'good', is prominent, occurring in verses 65 (*much kindness*), 66 (where the N.E.B. omits it as a repetition from the previous verse), 68 (*Thou art good and thou doest good*), 71 (*How good it is*), 72 (*means more to me*). For the first time in the psalm, the notion of *punishment* is introduced (verses 67, 71) which is seen as part of God's goodness, and the goodness of his commandments. *

Thy hands moulded me and made me what I am; 73
   show me how I may learn thy commandments.

Let all who fear thee be glad when they see me, 74
   because I hope for the fulfilment of thy word.

I know, O Lord, that thy decrees are just 75
   and even in punishing thou keepest faith with me.

Let thy never-failing love console me, 76
   as thou hast promised me, thy servant.

Extend thy compassion to me, that I may live; 77
   for thy law is my continual delight.

Put the proud to shame, for with their lies they wrong 78
     me;
   but I will meditate on thy precepts.

79 Let all who fear thee turn to me,
    all who cherish thy instruction.
80 Let me give my whole heart to thy statutes,
    so that I am not put to shame.

    ✻ 73–80. Verses *yōd*. The central thought is that vindication of
the psalmist by God will put the enemies to shame (verse 78)
and will be an encouragement to those who fear God (verses
74, 79). The psalmist has such confidence in God, who created
him and knows him intimately (verse 73), that he knows that
even when punishing him God is keeping faith (verse 75).
    79. *all who cherish:* the N.E.B. follows an ancient Hebrew
tradition which puts 79*b* in apposition to 79*a*. An alternative
tradition would mean 'in order that they may cherish . . .' ✻

81 I long with all my heart for thy deliverance,
    hoping for the fulfilment of thy word;
82 my sight grows dim with looking for thy promise
    and still I cry, 'When wilt thou comfort me?'
83 Though I shrivel like a wine-skin in the smoke,
    I do not forget thy statutes.
84 How long has thy servant to wait
    for thee to fulfil thy decree against my persecutors?
85 Proud men who flout thy law
    spread tales about me.
86 Help me, for they hound me with their lies,
    but thy commandments all stand for ever.
87 They had almost swept me from the earth,
    but I did not forsake thy precepts;
88 grant me life, as thy love is unchanging,
    that I may follow all thy instruction.

✻ 81–8. Verses *kap.* The psalmist reaches the depths of despair. His enemies have come close to gaining victory over him (verses 85–7), and although he does not waver from trust in God, he grows weary in his wait for vindication (verses 81f.) and desires to know when sentence will be given in his favour (verse 84).

81. *I long with all my heart:* literally 'my soul has wasted away waiting for deliverance'.

83. *wine-skin in the smoke:* a skin not used, and deteriorating from the smoke of the fire in the one-roomed house. ✻

Eternal is thy word, O Lord,   89
   planted firm in heaven.
Thy promise[a] endures for all time,   90
   stable as the earth which thou hast fixed.
This day, as ever, thy decrees stand fast;   91
   for all things serve thee.
If thy law had not been my continual delight,   92
   I should have perished in all my troubles;
never will I forget thy precepts,   93
   for through them thou hast given me life.
I am thine; O save me,   94
   for I have pondered thy precepts.
Evil men lie in wait to destroy me;   95
   but I will give thought to thy instruction.
I see that all things come to an end,   96
   but thy commandment has no limit.

✻ 89–96. Verses *lāmed.* God's revelation is linked to the created order in verses 89–91; his word, promise and decrees are as immovable as the created order, and all things created

[a] *Prob. rdg.; Heb.* Thy constancy.

serve God (verse 91*b*). Yet even earthly created things do not last for ever (verse 96) in contrast to God's commandment!

89. *planted firm:* the exact meaning of the Hebrew verb in this context is not certain. Literally 'Thy word O LORD stands for ever in heaven.' 'Word ' may here be God's eternal purposes.

90. *Thy promise:* since 'word' and *promise* go closely together in the psalm, the N.E.B. conjecture is here probably correct. Verses 89–90 are complementary, saying that God's 'word' and promise are as stable as heaven and earth.

91. There are several possible translations. The N.E.B. takes decrees as the object of *stand fast.* Another possibility is 'they (either heaven and earth or word and promise) stand fast according to thy decrees'.

96. A difficult first line, including a word that occurs only here in the Old Testament. The N.E.B. probably gets the general sense, which is a contrast between the limits of earthly things, and the limitlessness of God's commandments. ✷

97   O how I love thy law!
       It is my study all day long.

98   Thy commandments are mine for ever;
       through them I am wiser than my enemies.

99   I have more insight than all my teachers,
       for thy instruction is my study;

100   I have more wisdom than the old,
       because I have kept thy precepts.

101   I set no foot on any evil path
       in my obedience to thy word;

102   I do not swerve from thy decrees,
       for thou thyself hast been my teacher.

103   How sweet is thy promise in my mouth,
       sweeter on my tongue than honey!

From my precepts I learn wisdom;   104
    therefore I hate the paths of falsehood.

✻ 97–104. Verses *mēm*. The psalmist declares that in wisdom
and insight, he is superior to his enemies (verse 98) his teachers
(verse 99) and even to old men with a lifetime of experience
(verse 100). This is because his source of understanding has been
God's revelation (see especially verse 102*b*), studied and obeyed
continually (verse 97), and with single-minded devotion (verses
101f.). Yet this has not been a burdensome exercise, for the
things of God were sweeter than honey to the tongue (verse
103, and see Ps. 19: 10). ✻

Thy word is a lamp to guide my feet   105
    and a light on my path;
I have bound myself by oath and solemn vow   106
    to keep thy just decrees.
I am cruelly afflicted;   107
    O LORD, revive me and make good thy word.
Accept, O LORD, the willing tribute of my lips   108
    and teach me thy decrees.
Every day I take my life in my hands,   109
    yet I never forget thy law.
Evil men have set traps for me,   110
    but I do not stray from thy precepts.
Thy instruction is my everlasting inheritance;   111
    it is the joy of my heart.
I am resolved to fulfil thy statutes;   112
    they are a reward that never fails.

✻ 105–12. Verses *nūn*. The affliction of the psalmist by his
enemies once more comes to the fore (verses 107, 109f.). Each
day brings its risks, and it is as though he treads a path which is

cunningly set with traps by his enemies. In this situation, the psalmist is guided by God's word, which shows him the right path (verse 105).

105. *Thy word:* the term may include God's commandments (cp. 'the Ten Words', Deut. 4: 13) and the promises in written scriptures. *to guide my feet: my feet* may be an expression meaning the psalmist himself.

109. *I take my life in my hands:* literally 'my soul (life) is in my hand'; I risk my life.

112. *they are a reward:* or 'unto the end'. The same word is in verse 33. ✶

113 I hate men who are not single-minded,
    but I love thy law.
114 Thou art my shield and hiding-place;
    I hope for the fulfilment of thy word.
115 Go, you evildoers, and leave me to myself,
    that I may keep the commandments of my God.
116 Support me as thou hast promised, that I may live;
    do not disappoint my hope.
117 Sustain me, that I may see deliverance;
    so shall I always be occupied with thy statutes.
118 Thou dost reject those who stray from thy statutes,
    for their talk is all malice and lies.
119 In thy sight all the wicked on earth are scum;[a]
    therefore I love thy instruction.
120 The dread of thee makes my flesh creep,
    and I stand in awe of thy decrees.

✶ 113–20. Verses *sāmek*. A contrast is made between the psalmist who seeks to be loyal and wholehearted towards God,

[a] In . . . scum: *so some MSS.; others* Thou hast made an end of all the wicked on earth like scum.

and those who are not single-minded (verse 113), the evildoers (verse 115), those who stray from God's statutes (verse 118) and the wicked (verse 119). It is not easy to identify these people; are the wicked (verse 119) foreigners, Jews, or both? The identification affects the interpretation. If the evildoers are members of all nations, including Jews with little opportunity to know and observe God's laws, then there is an undoubted element of exclusivism in the section (e.g. verses 114f.).

113. *not single-minded:* the Hebrew word occurs only here in the Old Testament. It is not clear whether the psalmist's hate is directed towards the men themselves, or their double-minded, fickle attitude.

119. *scum:* is a vivid rendering of the Hebrew, which denotes the worthless remainder from the process of refining metals.

120. *makes my flesh creep:* the non-rational response to the eerie or unusual. ✱

I have done what is just and right;   121
    thou wilt not abandon me to my oppressors.
Stand surety for the welfare of thy servant;   122
    let not the proud oppress me.[a]
My sight grows dim with looking for thy deliverance   123
    and waiting for thy righteous promise.
In all thy dealings with me, Lord, show thy true love   124
    and teach me thy statutes.
I am thy servant; give me insight   125
    to understand thy instruction.
It is time to act, O Lord;   126
    for men have broken thy law.
Truly I love thy commandments   127
    more than the finest gold.

[a] oppress me: *or* charge me falsely.

128 It is by thy precepts*a* that I find the right way;
      I hate the paths of falsehood.

* 121–8. Verses *'āyin*. The psalmist is confident that God will
not abandon him (verse 121), but he has waited long (verse 123)
and he calls on God to act without delay (verses 126).

122. *Stand surety*: a legal term in Hebrew, implying that the
guarantor will be responsible for the person primarily liable.
Here, it is a strong way of asking God to be his protector.

126. This is a famous verse in Judaism, for one of its
interpretations was that the prophets had broken God's law in
order to act on his behalf (e.g. Elijah illegally built or rebuilt
the altar on Mount Carmel in order to bring the people back
to faith in God, 1 Kings 18: 30). It can be variously rendered:
'It is time to act for the LORD', or 'It is time for the LORD to
act' in addition to the N.E.B. rendering. *

129 Thy instruction is wonderful;
      therefore I gladly keep it.
130 Thy word is revealed, and all is light;
      it gives understanding even to the untaught.
131 I pant, I thirst,
      longing for thy commandments.
132 Turn to me and be gracious,
      as thou hast decreed for those who love thy name.
133 Make my step firm according to thy promise,
      and let no wrong have the mastery over me.
134 Set me free from man's oppression,
      that I may observe thy precepts.
135 Let thy face shine upon thy servant
      and teach me thy statutes.

[a] It . . . precepts: *prob. rdg., cp. Sept.; Heb.* All precepts of all.

Me eyes stream with tears   136
     because men do not heed thy law.

✻ 129–36. Verses *pē*. This section is partly the counterbalance
to verses 113–20. The psalmist is filled with indignation and
sorrow because men do not heed God's law (verse 136). This
reaction comes not only because such lawlessness hinders his
own obedience (verse 134) but because of the understanding
which God's word gives to the untaught (verse 130).

130. *Thy word is revealed:* literally 'the opening or entrance
(i.e. revelation) of thy words gives light'. The N.E.B. *word*
(instead of 'words') retains the special term in this psalm. Here
it probably includes the commandments and (written)
promises.

133. *Make my step firm:* i.e. direct my step. ✻

How just thou art, O Lord!   137
     How straight and true are thy decrees!
How just is the instruction thou givest!   138
     It is fixed firm and sure.
I am speechless with resentment,   139
     for my enemies have forgotten thy words.
Thy promise has been tested through and through,   140
     and thy servant loves it.
I may be despised and of little account,   141
     but I do not forget thy precepts.
Thy justice is an everlasting justice,   142
     and thy law is truth.
Though I am oppressed by trouble and anxiety,   143
     thy commandments are my continual delight.
Thy instruction is ever just;   144
     give me understanding that I may live.

✻ 137–44. Verses *ṣādē*. The justice, reality and truth of God's revelation (verses 137, 138, 140, 142, 144) are contrasted with the unimportance (verse 141) and frailty (verse 143) of the psalmist; but this contrast is a ground for hope.

139. *I am speechless with resentment*: literally 'my zeal has cut me off (consumed me)'. The psalmist's burning loyalty to God is the cause of his attitude to the enemies who have forgotten God's words. ✻

145 I call with my whole heart; answer me, LORD.
    I will keep thy statutes.
146 I call to thee; O save me
    that I may heed thy instruction.
147 I rise before dawn and cry for help;
    I hope for the fulfilment of thy word.
148 Before the midnight watch also my eyes are open
    for meditation on thy promise.
149 Hear me, as thy love is unchanging,
    and give me life, O LORD, by thy decree.
150 My pursuers in their malice are close behind me,
    but they are far from thy law.
151 Yet thou art near, O LORD,
    and all thy commandments are true.
152 I have long known from thy instruction
    that thou hast given it eternal foundations.

✻ 145–52. Verses *qōp*. Fervent prayers to God for his assistance (verses 145–9) end in the confident assertion that God is near (verse 151). While God is close to the psalmist, the enemies are far from God's law (verse 150). ✻

153 See in what trouble I am and set me free,
    for I do not forget thy law.

Be thou my advocate and win release for me;   154
   true to thy promise, give me life.

Such deliverance is beyond the reach of wicked men,   155
because they do not ponder thy statutes.

Great is thy compassion, O LORD;   156
   grant me life by thy decree.

Many are my persecutors and enemies,   157
   but I have not swerved from thy instruction.

I was cut to the quick when I saw traitors   158
   who had no regard for thy promise.

See how I love thy precepts, O LORD!   159
   Grant me life, as thy love is unchanging.

Thy word is founded in truth,   160
   and thy just decrees are everlasting.

✷ 153–69. Verses *rēsh*. This section repeats the themes of the
psalmist's oppression (verses 153, 155, 157), and his prayer to
God for deliverance (verses 154, 156, 159). ✷

The powers that be persecute me without cause,   161
   yet my heart thrills at thy word.

I am jubilant over thy promise,   162
   like a man carrying off much booty.

Falsehood I detest and loathe,   163
   but I love thy law.

Seven times a day I praise thee   164
   for the justice of thy decrees.

Peace is the reward of those who love thy law;   165
   no pitfalls beset their path.

I hope for thy deliverance, O LORD,   166
   and I fulfil thy commandments;

167 gladly I heed thy instruction
        and love it greatly.
168 I heed thy precepts and thy instruction,
        for all my life lies open before thee.

⁜ 161–8. Verses *shīn*. The psalmist's joy and gladness in
receiving and obeying God's revelation, are prominent in this
section.

161. *my heart thrills*: literally 'my heart is afraid'. The N.E.B.
presumably means the sort of thrill that comes from that
which is awesome.

165. *Peace is the reward*: it is clear from the psalm that peace
in the sense of freedom from oppression and anxiety is *not*
meant. Here, it may mean a wholesome relationship with God,
and the inner strength which comes from this. ⁜

169 Let my cry of joy reach thee, O LORD;
        give me understanding of[a] thy word.
170 Let my supplication reach thee;
        be true to thy promise and save me.
171 Let thy praise pour from my lips,
        because thou teachest me thy statutes;
172 let the music of thy promises be on my tongue,
        for thy commandments are justice itself.
173 Let thy hand be prompt to help me,
        for I have chosen thy precepts;
174 I long for thy deliverance, O LORD,
        and thy law is my continual delight.
175 Let me live and I will praise thee;
        let thy decrees be my support.
176 I have strayed like a lost sheep;

[a] of: *so some MSS.; others* in fulfilment of.

come, search for thy servant,
for I have not forgotten thy commandments.

✻ 169–76. Verses *tāw*. This remarkable psalm ends (verse 176)
with the psalmist's confession that he is like a sheep who has
gone astray. He prays once more for deliverance from his
enemies (verses 174f.) and seeks God's assistance for his
attempts at worship and praise (verses 169f.). Thus the final
impression is one of great honesty and humility on the
psalmist's part. He does not say, 'follow me along the path of
obedience', but 'there is the path that is just, true and enduring,
along which, with God's help, we may stumble together'. ✻

I SOUGHT PEACE – THEY WERE FOR WAR

120

I called to the LORD in my distress,	1
and he answered me.	
'O LORD,' I cried, 'save me from lying lips	2
and from the tongue of slander.'	
What has he in store for you, slanderous tongue?	3
What more has he for you?	
Nothing but a warrior's sharp arrows	4
or red-hot charcoal.[a]	
Hard is my lot, exiled in Meshech,	5
dwelling by the tents of Kedar.	
All the time that I dwelt	6
among men who hated peace,	
I sought peace; but whenever I spoke of it,	7
they were for war.	

[a] *Lit.* or live coals of desert broom.

✻ This is the first of fifteen psalms (120–134) entitled in the Hebrew 'A song of ascents'. The meaning of this title is not known, but the most probable explanation is that these psalms were used on the occasion of pilgrimages to Jerusalem. Pss. 121, 122, 125, 127 certainly suggest, from their content, that they would be suitable for such occasions.

The main question affecting the interpretation of this psalm is whether verses 5–7 describe an actual or a metaphorical exile. The N.E.B. appears to support the former, although the simplest theory is that the whole passage about exile is metaphorical. The psalmist's neighbours had mistaken his peaceful intentions (verse 7), perhaps mistaken them for weakness, and attacked him, especially with the weapon of false accusation (verse 2). But the psalmist asserts his belief in God's justice, and that his slanderers will be punished (verses 3f.). A date is impossible to determine.

1. *I called:* the tenses may either be taken as past, so that the psalmist is looking back to past experience, or they may be present, and thus represent a present cry for help.

2. *lying lips:* the lips and tongue of the psalmist's enemies.

3. *What has he in store for you:* the subject of the verbs is God, and the verse presupposes the oath formula as at 1 Kings 19: 2 ('The gods do the same to me and more, unless by this time tomorrow I have taken your life as you took theirs'). What the enemies swear to do to the psalmist will, through God's justice, be done to the enemies.

4. This verse would appear to state what the enemies purposed to do to the psalmist.

5. *exiled in Meshech:* Meshech is usually understood to be a people, or country, near the Black Sea (see Gen. 10: 2), while Kedar (Gen. 25: 13) was probably a people inhabiting the Syro-Arabian desert. The fact that these two places are so far apart has led some interpreters to understand the exile as a metaphorical exile, expressive of the psalmist's distress (verses 1f.). Alternatively, other editors alter *Meshech* to the name of a place nearer to Kedar.

6f. A reminder that reconciliation may be mistaken for weakness, and that to be a peacemaker often involves pain. ✻

THE LORD IS YOUR GUARDIAN

121

If I lift up my eyes to the hills,   1
   where shall I find help?
Help[a] comes only from the LORD,   2
   maker of heaven and earth.

How could he let your foot stumble?   3
   How could he, your guardian, sleep?
The guardian of Israel   4
   never slumbers, never sleeps.

The LORD is your guardian,   5
   your defence at your right hand;
the sun will not strike you by day   6
   nor the moon by night.

The LORD will guard you against all evil;   7
   he will guard you, body and soul.
The LORD will guard your going and your coming,   8
   now and for evermore.

✻ This well-known psalm is a beautiful expression of faith in God's care and protection. It is the counterpart to Ps. 120. Like other psalms with the same content (e.g. Ps. 91) it does not imply that ancient Israelites expected to be completely free from adversity. Scholars are divided as to whether the psalm is one for a procession towards, and entry into, Jerusalem, or whether it is rather the blessing given when a pilgrim leaves the holy places. Attempts have been made to show that the psalm was originally antiphonal, with verses 1 and 3 questions

[a] *Lit.* My help.

from the worshipper, and verses 2 and 4 answers from the priest. The very divergence of scholarly opinion shows that objective criteria for such reconstructions are lacking. A date is impossible to determine.

1. Either the whole verse can be a question, as in the N.E.B., or 1*a* can be a statement, and 1*b* a question. The hills may be those on which Jerusalem is built; or the psalmist may gaze apprehensively at the hills to be crossed on his homeward journey, asking as he looks, how he will get help on the way home.

2. *Help comes:* the N.E.B., which prefers *Help* to 'My help', implies that the psalmist's question is answered by another person, e.g. a priest. The Hebrew would imply that the psalmist answers his own question. The divine helper is the *maker of heaven and earth.*

3. This verse certainly seems to begin a greeting or parting blessing uttered by a cultic official. *How could he:* translators are divided on whether verse 3 is a rhetorical question implying the answer 'no' (so the N.E.B.), a wish, 'may he not let your foot stumble . . .' or a statement, 'he will not let your foot stumble . . .' *guardian:* one who keeps constant watch in order to protect his charge. This constant watchfulness is fully described in verse 4.

5. *your defence:* literally 'shade' – the image is that of protection from the blazing heat of the sun – see verse 6. *right hand:* the position of favour and trust; cp. Ps. 110: 1.

6. The moon, as well as the sun, was believed to have harmful effects.

7. *body and soul:* the N.E.B. makes it clear that the reference is to the whole person.

8. *going and . . . coming:* literally 'going out and coming in' meaning entering and leaving the temple for the pilgrimage, and daily work and affairs in the future. ✻

PRAY FOR THE PEACE OF JERUSALEM

122

I rejoiced when they said to me,   1
  'Let us go to the house of the LORD.'
Now we stand within your gates,   2
  O Jerusalem:
Jerusalem that is built to be a city   3
  where people come together in unity;
to which the tribes resort, the tribes of the LORD,   4
  to give thanks to the LORD himself,
  the bounden duty of Israel.
For in her are set the thrones of justice,   5
  the thrones of the house of David.
Pray for the peace of Jerusalem: 6
  'May those who love you prosper;
peace be within your ramparts   7
  and prosperity in your palaces.'
For the sake of these my brothers and my friends,   8
  I will say, 'Peace be within you.'
For the sake of the house of the LORD our God   9
  I will pray for your good.

✴ This psalm is clearly a composition connected with pilgrimage to Jerusalem. Whether is was used by pilgrims on arrival, or whether it is a reflection by a pilgrim who has returned home, depends on the interpretation of verse 2. We cannot be certain that it was used for a particular festival (e.g. Tabernacles); it could just as well have been a general pilgrimage psalm (but see on verse 4). The psalm has been dated anywhere between the time of David (about 1000 B.C.) and the time of Nehemiah (fifth century B.C.). This depends on whether verse 5 implies that a Davidic king is ruling; the alternative is that the functions of the Davidic throne are continued after the exile, but not in the institution of kingship. In a larger context of interpretation, the psalm is not only a prayer for blessing on Jerusalem, but a prayer for the universal peace and justice that will follow from the establishment of the kingdom of God, of which Jerusalem and the house of David are symbols.

1. *'Let us go . . .':* if the psalm concerns a regular (annual) pilgrimage, this phrase may be a formula that was recited as preparations were made, or as the journey was commenced (cp. Isa. 2: 3).

2. *Now we stand:* literally 'our feet were standing'. The N.E.B. assumes that the Hebrew denotes more the lasting quality of the action, than its temporal aspect. If we take the verbs to be referring to the past, then the pilgrim has returned home, and is reflecting on his journey.

3. *where people come together in unity:* the Hebrew 'joined for itself together' is very cryptic, and it is not clear whether the reference is to the manner in which the city is built (cp. Ps. 48: 12) or to its actual and symbolical function in achieving the unity of the Israelite people.

4. *to which the tribes resort:* it is difficult to know whether actual or idealized practice is described. Probably during the reigns of David and Solomon, all of the tribes did go up to Jerusalem, but how far this remained true after the division of the kingdom at Solomon's death is uncertain. *to the LORD himself:* Hebrew 'to the name of the LORD'. 'Name' here is a way of saying that God has placed his presence in Jerusalem (Deut. 12: 11). *bounden duty:* this is usually linked with Exod. 23: 14–17, the regulation that all males must appear before God at the sanctuary at three principal festivals. This may mean that the psalm is to be connected with all or one of these festivals, unless we regard verses 3–5 as a recapitulation of the glories of Jerusalem, in which the psalmist is not necessarily a participant.

5. The king (possibly assisted by his family) constituted the

highest court, and probably a court of appeal (2 Sam. 14: 4–20; 15: 3f.).

6. There seems to be play upon the similar sounds of the Hebrew words for 'peace' (*shalom*) and the 'salem' part of Jerusalem. *peace* is rendered by some translators as 'prosperity', but these two different words appear in verses 6 and 7. The N.E.B. takes 6b–7 as the content of the prayer for Jerusalem.

8f. The psalmist appears to pray not only for Jerusalem as a city, but for those, his *brothers and . . . friends*, who dwell there. Ultimately, if the inhabitants of Jerusalem enjoy peace and prosperity, this will mean safety for the house of God, the rationale of Jerusalem's existence. ✶

DEAL KINDLY WITH US, O LORD

123

I lift my eyes to thee   1
    whose throne is in heaven.
As the eyes of a slave follow his master's hand   2
    or the eyes of a slave-girl her mistress,
    so our eyes are turned to the LORD our God
    waiting for kindness from him.
Deal kindly with us, O LORD, deal kindly,   3
    for we have suffered insult enough;
too long have we had to suffer   4
    the insults of the wealthy,
    the scorn of proud men.

✶ An individual, or a representative of the community (note the 'I' in verse 1 and the 'we' in verses 2–4), prays for deliverance. The circumstances cannot be determined. The psalm may date from the exile, or from the time of Nehemiah.

1. *I lift my eyes:* literally 'I have lifted up my eyes' (and continue to do so). The persistence of the psalmist's hope is

emphasized. *whose throne is in heaven:* the psalm emphasizes the universal power and might of God (see also verse 2).

2–4. Interpreters are divided over whether the hand of the master and mistress (the N.E.B. paraphrases the second line, omitting reference to the hand of the mistress) is a way of speaking about the power of the ruler, or whether the hand is watched so that its every gesture is obeyed. The N.E.B. seems to favour the second possibility, while the first suggestion could be paraphrased 'as the slave is dependent upon his master . . .' It is not clear whether the psalmist thinks that his misfortunes have come from God, just as a master had the right to punish his slave; but, however the relation is conceived, God is not one who will be unmoved by the psalmist's prayer, and the psalmist looks upward in confident hope of gracious dealing from his master. ✷

IF THE LORD HAD NOT BEEN ON OUR SIDE

124

1   If the LORD had not been on our side,
       Israel may now say,

2   if the LORD had not been on our side
       when they assailed us,

3   they would have swallowed us alive
       when their anger was roused against us.

4   The waters would have carried us away
       and the torrent swept over us;

5   over us would have swept
       the seething waters.

6   Blessed be the LORD, who did not leave us
       to be the prey between their teeth.

7   We have escaped like a bird
       from the fowler's trap;

> the trap broke, and so we escaped.
> Our help is in the name of the LORD,   8
> maker of heaven and earth.

✻ This psalm is a hymn of deliverance uttered by Israel (verse 1) apparently on the occasion of escape from an enemy. The psalmist employs several figures in order to describe the calamity. In verses 2f., the figure is that of swift military attack, in verses 4f. the enemy is described as a raging torrent; in verse 6 the adversary is like a wild animal seeking prey, and in verse 7 is like a skilled hunter. The very variety of metaphors suggests that the use of the psalm could extend to many occasions of distress. The psalm is an affirmation of the eternal vigilance for his people on the part of God, the 'maker of heaven and earth' (verse 8). A date is difficult to determine.

1f. The force of the Hebrew is 'If it had been anyone else but the LORD on our side . . . they would have swallowed us . . .' The repetition of the opening line gives added emphasis (and cp. Ps. 129: 1f. for a similar use of repetition).

3. *they would have swallowed us:* this may be a way of describing overwhelming victory, or the background may be that of the swallowing of victims by the earth (Num. 16: 30), by Sheol (Prov. 1: 12) or by a monster (Jer. 51: 34).

4f. The torrents suggest an unexpected and overwhelming foe; but in the psalms, God is master of the raging torrents (Ps. 93: 3f.).

7f. The bird could not break free from the trap unaided; thus, Israel's deliverance also depended upon the help of another, the God who made *heaven and earth*. ✻

PEACE BE UPON ISRAEL

125

Those who trust in the LORD are like Mount Zion,   1
which cannot be shaken but stands fast for ever.

2 As the hills enfold Jerusalem,
  so the LORD enfolds his people, now and evermore.
3 The sceptre of wickedness shall surely find no home
      in the land allotted to the righteous,
  so that the righteous shall not set
      their hands to injustice.
4 Do good, O LORD, to those who are good
      and to those who are upright in heart.
5 But those who turn aside into crooked ways,
  may the LORD destroy them, as he destroys all evildoers!

  Peace be upon Israel!

✳ The psalm falls into two main parts. In verses 1f., there is
an affirmation of confidence in God's eternal power to protect his people, especially those who trust in him. Verse 3
directs itself to a specific situation of distress, which seems to
be the occasion of the psalm's composition. There follows a
prayer that, in this distress, God will redeem the righteous and
confound the wicked: that his general care for his people
will be manifested in this particular instance. The nature of the
distress and the date of the psalm cannot be determined.

  1. That *Mount Zion . . . cannot be shaken* when the world
is in tumult is a theme found also in Ps. 46: 5. Here, the im-
movability of Zion is a figure for stability in trouble, for
Those who trust in the LORD.

  2. The psalmist moves from the impregnable city, to the
hills which surround it. These, in turn, become a symbol for
God's surrounding protection for his people.

  3. *The sceptre of wickedness* denotes the power of a foreign
nation, or of a godless party within Israel. *surely find no home:*
this implies that the foreign power or alien party at present
holds sway in Israel, but that this will not be a permanent
state of affairs. *the land allotted to the righteous:* this is the

promised land, and the allusion is to the apportionment of the land in the time of Moses and Joshua (cp. Josh. 13: 1). If *righteous* means Israel as a whole in this context, it is to be noted that this righteousness is God's gift, and not Israel's achievement. *so that the righteous . . . to injustice:* the sense seems to be that if God did allow wickedness to rule permanently in the land, the righteous (i.e. Israel) would cease to be righteous, for they would be driven to that desperation in which they would *set their hands to injustice.* God will not permit his people to be tested beyond what they can bear (cp. 1 Cor. 10: 13).

4. *Do good . . . who are good:* the N.E.B. brings out the pun on 'good' in the Hebrew. Verses 4 and 5 raise for the modern reader the question why some men are good and *upright in heart,* and others *turn aside into crooked ways*; but if the psalmist is aware of the dilemma, he does not comment upon it. He wishes to affirm his belief in the ultimate justice of God, which will surely be seen in the appropriate rewards and punishments received by men.

5. *Peace be upon Israel!:* not merely a request for absence of conflict, but a desire that in every way, Israel should prosper. *

GREAT THINGS INDEED THE LORD THEN DID FOR US

126

When the LORD turned the tide of Zion's fortune,   1
   we were like men who had found new health.[a]
Our mouths were full of laughter   2
   and our tongues sang aloud for joy.
Then word went round among the nations,
   'The LORD has done great things for them.'
Great things indeed the LORD then did for us,   3
   and we rejoiced.

[a] like . . . health: *or* like dreamers.

4   Turn once again our fortune, LORD,
           as streams return in the dry south.[a]

5   Those who sow in tears
           shall reap with songs of joy.

6   A man may go out weeping,
           carrying his bag of seed;
       but he will come back with songs of joy,
           carrying home his sheaves.

* There are two major ways of interpreting this psalm. Verses 1–3 may be taken as looking forward to a future restoration, i.e. 'When the LORD turns the tide . . . we shall be like men . . .' Verses 4–6 will then be a prayer that God will speedily accomplish the restoration, the psalmist being sustained by the thought that the prayer will be answered as surely as the toil of sowing is rewarded by the joy of harvesting (verses 5f.). The second approach is reflected in the N.E.B. translation and is the more probable interpretation. Verses 1–3 refer to a past restoration, most probably the return from the Babylonian exile in 540 B.C. The request in verse 4 is then that God will help the Israelites in Jerusalem, who are suffering undisclosed difficulties. In this case, the psalm will have been composed after the exile. It is just possible that the psalm was a prayer for God's blessing upon agriculture, used at a New Year festival.

1. *When the LORD turned:* the philological basis of the phrase has been much discussed; however it is rendered, it most probably refers to the return from the Babylonian exile, though it may originally have denoted more generally a change of fortune. *Zion* indicates that Israel is a religious community whose visible sign of unity is Jerusalem and its temple (see Ps. 122: 3). *found new health:* whether this, or the translation in the footnote is the more correct, the point

[a] dry south: *Heb.* Negeb.

remains that God's act was amazing for those whom it affected directly or indirectly.

2. *mouths . . . tongues:* Hebrew idiom for the whole person.

4. *as streams return:* with the autumn and winter rains, which fill the dry *wadi* courses. The *dry south* is the region to the south of Judah. The Hebrew word (N.E.B. footnote) is used today to denote the desert south of modern Israel.

5f. Some interpreters regard these words as words of comfort spoken by a cultic official. Alternatively, they continue the prayer of verse 4, and are a reminder to God and to the psalmist of the rejoicing which certainly replaces the toil of sowing and tending the crops. Deliverance will come as surely as the people are now in distress. *tears . . . weeping:* these may have been ritually associated with sowing and planting, though we cannot know whether this was simply custom, or thought to have causative effects on the harvest. *go out weeping* could simply be an expression for the undoubted hard work in agriculture in those times. ✲

UNLESS THE LORD BUILDS THE HOUSE

127

Unless the LORD builds the house, 1
its builders will have toiled in vain.
Unless the LORD keeps watch over a city,
in vain the watchman stands on guard.
In vain you rise up early 2
and go late to rest,
toiling for the bread you eat;
he supplies the need of those he loves.[a]
Sons are a gift from the LORD 3
and children a reward from him.
Like arrows in the hand of a fighting man 4

[a] *Prob. rdg.; Heb. adds an unintelligible word.*

> are the sons of a man's youth.
> 5   Happy is the man
>   who has his quiver full of them;
>   such men shall not be put to shame
>   when they confront their enemies in court.[a]

✻ This psalm begins by stating in general that God must be the initiator and sustainer of any enterprise that is to endure (verses 1f.). It then refers by implication to the god-fearing man, whose reward it is to have a large family. Among numerous benefits of having many sons will be the ease of obtaining justice in court (see on verse 5). The second part of the psalm complements the first part. One practical way in which God builds and sustains a house is by granting abundant posterity to the faithful. The date and original setting of the psalm are difficult to determine. In Christian worship its contents have made it seem appropriate for the services of dedication of church buildings, and of thanksgiving after childbirth.

1. *Unless the LORD builds the house: house* is probably used in a wide sense, which could include the temple, an ordinary house, or a dynasty or family. *keeps watch:* the divine involvement cannot end when the erection of a structure is completed: his unceasing care is also necessary.

2. The persons addressed appear to be those who toil anxiously from early morning to late evening seeking their livelihood, but without trust in God. The last line is a problem, and in addition to the N.E.B. rendering, it has been interpreted 'for all these things he supplies to those he loves as they sleep' or 'he gives (children) to those he loves, in sleep (= marital intercourse)'. However the line is taken, it makes a contrast between fruitless human toil, and God's gracious gifts. The verse as a whole condemns, not hard work, but anxious toil that leaves God out of account (and cp. the advice

[a] *Lit.* in the gate.

in the New Testament 'put away anxious thoughts', Matt.
6: 25). *those he loves* follows the Septuagint. The Hebrew is
'his beloved', no doubt a reference to Solomon with whom
the psalm is associated in later Jewish exegesis, as in the psalm
title, 'of Solomon'.

3–6. In an agricultural society, a large number of children
will help to defend and work the family lands. The psalmist,
however, sees the greatest benefit as accruing in the field of
justice, where cases were heard in the gate of the city (cp.
the N.E.B. footnote). Whereas in corrupt times justice might
be denied to the defenceless (e.g. the widow and orphan) it
would hardly be denied to a man backed by a number of hefty
sons! It is less likely that the passage refers to actual fighting or
feuding between families. ✶

HAPPY ARE ALL THEY WHO FEAR THE LORD

128

Happy are all who fear the LORD,   1
    who live according to his will.
You shall eat the fruit of your own labours,   2
    you shall be happy and you shall prosper.
Your wife shall be like a fruitful vine   3
    in the heart of your house;
your sons shall be like olive-shoots
    round about your table.
This is the blessing in store for the man   4
    who fears the LORD.
May the LORD bless you from Zion;   5
    may you share the prosperity of Jerusalem
all the days of your life,
    and live to see your children's children!   6

Peace be upon Israel!

* Like the second part of Ps. 127, this psalm describes the blessings enjoyed by the god-fearing man, in terms of abundant offspring. Although it is possible to suggest a number of appropriate settings for the psalm's original composition – a wedding, a pilgrimage to Zion, a general blessing at a major festival – no certainty is possible. The psalm appears to consist mainly of an address or blessing by a teacher or cultic official, prefaced by a general statement. It differs from Ps. 127 in that it stresses the companionship and joys expressed within the family circle (verse 3). The blessing enjoyed by the family will overflow into the general prosperity of Jerusalem and Israel (verses 5f.).

1. Cp. Pss. 1: 1 and 119: 1. *who live . . .:* Hebrew 'who walk in his ways'.

2. *You shall eat:* it did not follow in ancient Israel that a man would always enjoy the fruit of his labours on the land. Deprivation by an enemy nation, or drought, or disease, or a plague of locusts, could be his lot from time to time. The Israelites tended to regard such disasters as God's punishment, something that would pass by a truly god-fearing man, although the destiny of the individual was obviously bound up with that of the community (and note verses 5f.).

3. Two images are brought together: the table suggests the joys of family life, as the god-fearing man presides over meals. The vine suggests the vitality and beauty of the wife, who achieves a close and harmonious relationship with her numerous children, who are symbolized by *olive-shoots.*

5. *May the LORD . . .:* or 'May the LORD who dwells in Zion bless you.' *share the prosperity:* the individual cannot prosper apart from his community; thus this is also a prayer for Jerusalem (cp. Ps. 122: 6f.).

6. *Peace:* see on Ps. 125: 5. *

LET ALL THE ENEMIES OF ZION
BE THROWN BACK IN SHAME

129

Often since I was young have men attacked me –   1
  let Israel now say –
often since I was young have men attacked me,   2
  but never have they prevailed.
They scored my back with scourges,   3
  like ploughmen driving long furrows.
Yet the LORD in his justice   4
  has cut me loose from the bonds of the wicked.
Let all enemies of Zion   5
  be thrown back in shame;
let them be like grass growing on the roof,   6
  which withers before it can shoot,
which will never fill a mower's hand   7
  nor yield an armful for the harvester,
so that passers-by will never say to them,   8
  'The blessing of the LORD be upon you!
  We bless you in the name of the LORD.'

✳ This psalm is reminiscent of Ps. 124. Both psalms contain
the phrase 'Israel may now say' or 'let Israel now say'
(124: 1f.; 129: 1f.) followed by a repetition of the opening
line, and both speak of God's deliverance of his people from
their enemies. However, Ps. 124 concludes with a hymn of
praise to God, with Israel speaking in the first person plural,
while Ps. 129 concludes with an imprecation (but see below)
against the enemies of Israel, Israel speaking in the first person
singular. Translators are divided on whether verses 5–8 are
an imprecation, or a statement which sees the outworking of
God's justice (verse 4) resulting in the certain defeat of

Israel's enemies. The N.E.B. translates the verses as an imprecation, but although this reveals the frailty and humanity of
Israel, the imprecation is a prayer that God's age-old purposes
for Israel should continue to triumph (see on verses 6f. below). The date and setting of the psalm are impossible to
determine, though it may well presuppose the Babylonian
exile and the return.

1f. *Often since I was young:* suggesting Israel's 'adoption'
by God as a son at the exodus (Hos. 11: 1). The period of the
judges and onwards would furnish many instances of attack
against Israel. The repetition of the phrase adds emphasis
(cp. Ps. 124: 1f.). *never have they prevailed:* the oppression by a
foreign nation may have lasted for several generations, but
it was never permanent. The problems of a single generation
must not be thought to reflect the whole of reality.

3. Hebrew 'Ploughmen ploughed my back; they made
their furrows long.' The N.E.B. is a paraphrase which tries
to draw out the two ideas implied in the Hebrew, that of
severe injuries inflicted upon the back of the victim, and that
of the ploughman whose long furrows disfigure the smooth
surface of a field.

4. *the LORD in his justice:* this phrase is difficult to translate
adequately. It certainly means more than 'the LORD is righteous' (Authorized Version, Revised Version, Revised Standard
Version) and the N.E.B. rightly brings an active sense into
the translation. *cut me loose:* the image has possibly changed to
that of Israel as an animal yoked for long servitude.

5. This verse, and the following verses, may also be taken
as a statement – 'All enemies of Zion will be thrown back in
shame.' If the interpretation of verses 1f. offered above is
correct, the *enemies of Zion* can hardly be other than foreign
nations; but see verse 8.

6f. The desire that the enemies should flourish as little as
grass on a flat roof that never becomes established, is another
way of expressing what is asserted in verse 2, that the enemies
in the past have never prevailed. The prayer is thus not so

much a malicious wish directed against enemies, as a prayer for the continued success of God's age-long purposes for Israel.

8. The connection of this verse with what precedes is not easy. It is probably best to regard it as being connected with the image of harvesting from verses 6f., but the enemies are no longer the grass, but the harvester, whose success is so minimal that the traditional greetings of the harvesters (Ruth 2: 4) are withheld. If, as some interpreters suggest, the enemies are not necessarily foreign nations, but certain groups within Israel, this might ease the difficulty that the blessing to be withheld from the enemy (foreign nation) is a blessing in the name of the LORD. However, against this, see on verse 5. Indeed, the difficulty of interpreting this psalm arises from the remarkable way in which it brings together many different images, shifting from one to the other in kaleidoscopic fashion. *

O ISRAEL, LOOK FOR THE LORD

130

Out of the depths have I called to thee, O LORD;	1
Lord, hear my cry.	
Let thy ears be attentive	2
to my plea for mercy.	
If thou, LORD, shouldest keep account of sins,	3
who, O Lord, could hold up his head?	
But in thee is forgiveness,	4
and therefore thou art revered.	
I wait for the LORD with all my soul,	5
I hope for the fulfilment of his word.	
My soul waits[a] for the Lord	6
more eagerly than watchmen for the morning.	

[a] waits: *transposed from after* the LORD *in verse 5.*

Like men who watch for the morning,
7   O Israel, look for the LORD.
For in the LORD is love unfailing,
           and great is his power to set men free.
8   He alone will set Israel free
           from all their sins.

✻ The major difficulty of interpretation in this psalm is the
relationship between verses 1–6 and 7f. Verses 1–6 appear to
be the cry of an individual, while verses 7f. exhort Israel as a
whole to trust in God. Many explanations have been advan-
ced, for example, that verses 7f. are a later addition; that the
'I' of verses 1–6 is Israel personified; that the individual of
verses 1–6 addresses the congregation in verses 7f.; that the
individual worshipper recalls in verses 7f. a congregational
formula. However the psalm reached its present form, it is
clear that in this form it is appropriate for either individual or
congregational use, and further speculation can be based on no
firm criteria. In Christian tradition, this is a Penitential psalm.
    1. *Out of the depths:* i.e. depths of waters, which symbolize
danger and distress (and cp. the cry of distress of Jonah from
the depths, Jonah 2: 2–5). No doubt the verse could apply to
many situations, including illness, and feelings of spiritual
estrangement from God.
    2. *Lord:* in verses 1–3 there is an alternation between the
divine names *Yahweh* and *Yah* (LORD), and *'adonai* (Lord),
the latter possibly suggesting the status of a servant before his
master. Both clauses in verse 2 are governed by 'Lord' in
this possible sense.
    3f. If 'Lord' does suggest a servant–master relationship,
it is made clear that God is no ordinary master. Although it
is in his power to keep a strict *account of sins*, his essential
nature is to forgive (this is the sense of *in thee is forgiveness*).
No human person could survive if he were duly punished for
all his sins. The effect of God's forgiveness is not encourage-

ment to sin all the more, but the creation of reverence – a combination of awe, fear and love. *hold up his head:* Hebrew 'stand'. It is arguable that the N.E.B. is not strong enough here; the verses are not about losing face (if that is what the N.E.B. means to convey), but about the impossibility of a man's survival if God takes strict account of sin. Some interpreters connect the 'stand' of this line with the 'stand' of the so-called entrance liturgies (e.g. Ps. 24: 3).

5–7. These verses present several textual problems, solution of which is not generally agreed. The N.E.B. takes the repeated phrase *men who watch for the morning* (verse 6c) as the beginning of a new sentence. Others omit it as having been copied twice, or take it closely with 6b, regarding it as a repetition for the sake of emphasis. The Hebrew of verse 5a is literally 'I wait for the LORD, my soul waits (for him).' The N.E.B. transposes *waits* in order to provide a verb for 6a, which otherwise lacks a verb in the Hebrew. Another possibility is to follow the Hebrew manuscript from Cave 11 of Qumran, in which there is a verb for 6a, meaning wait or trust, but derived from a different stem from the verb rendered *wait* in verse 5. This then makes it unnecessary to alter verse 5. Whatever solution is adopted, the general sense is clear – the psalmist waits in hope and expectancy for God to grant deliverance in accordance with his word (verse 5) and his nature to forgive (verse 4).

7f. *in the LORD:* this balances verse 4, 'in thee is forgiveness' perhaps suggesting the unity of the psalm. *He alone:* the Hebrew is emphatic that God alone can deliver Israel. Thus the psalmist and the community must wait and trust, not turning to any substitute that will have no power to set men free. ✳

I SUBMIT MYSELF

131

1   O Lord, my heart is not proud,
        nor are my eyes haughty;
      I do not busy myself with great matters
        or things too marvellous for me.
2   No; I submit myself, I account myself lowly
        as a weaned child clinging to its mother.[a]
3   O Israel, look for the Lord
        now and evermore.

✻ At first sight, this is a self-righteous utterance which seems
to have no point other than to commend the psalmist to God
and his fellows. However, most interpreters see in verse 2 an
expression of a very close relationship with God, from which
the psalmist has learned to live within his capabilities and to
be satisfied with his lot (verse 1). Though one might wish the
piety of this psalm to be a little more 'muscular', it is essentially the utterance of a man who has come to terms with himself. We would be wrong to conclude from verse 1 that the
psalmist takes no part in social and communal life; his ambition is to serve God first, and to serve his community as a
servant of God. A date is difficult to determine.

1. A 'proud heart' and 'haughty eyes' are signs of ambition
achieved or desired, together with contempt for one's fellow
men. All such attitudes are foreign to the psalmist. *things too
marvellous:* in the sense of 'too difficult'. Perhaps the psalmist
is denying that he would ever aspire to do what only God
can do.

2. The N.E.B. is a paraphrase of the Hebrew 'I (have)
levelled, I (have) silenced my soul', which presumably means
something like coming to terms with oneself by no longer

[a] *Prob. rdg.; Heb. adds* as a weaned child clinging to me.

entertaining impossible ambitions. It is difficult to know
whether the comparison with the weaned child is a symbol of
contentment, or whether it expresses the sort of relationship
in which the one who has become free is still dependent. The
weaned child is in one sense free from dependence upon its
mother, but it may still long for its mother's breast, a symbol
of man as independent, but holding to God.

3. The psalm closes with an exhortation to Israel (which is
not necessarily only the worshipping community in Jerusalem) to seek similar dependence upon God. ✲

REJECT NOT THINE ANOINTED KING

132

O Lord, remember David	1
in the time of his adversity,	
how he swore to the Lord	2
and made a vow to the Mighty One of Jacob:	
'I will not enter my house	3
nor will I mount my bed,	
I will not close my eyes in sleep	4
or my eyelids in slumber,	
until I find a sanctuary for the Lord,	5
a dwelling for the Mighty One of Jacob.'	
We heard of it in Ephrathah;	6
we came upon it in the region of Jaar.	
Let us enter his dwelling,	7
let us fall in worship at his footstool.	
Arise, O Lord, and come to thy resting-place,	8
thou and the ark of thy power.	
Let thy priests be clothed in righteousness	9
and let thy loyal servants shout for joy.	
For thy servant David's sake	10

reject not thy anointed king.

11 The LORD swore to David
  an oath which he will not break:
'A prince of your own line
  will I set upon your throne

12 If your sons keep my covenant
  and heed the teaching that I give them,
their sons in turn for all time
  shall sit upon your throne.'

13 For the LORD has chosen Zion
  and desired it for his home:

14 'This is my resting-place for ever;
  here will I make my home, for such is my desire.

15 I will richly bless her destitute[a]
  and satisfy her needy with bread.

16 With salvation will I clothe her priests;
  her loyal servants shall shout for joy.

17 There will I renew the line of[b] David's house
  and light a lamp for my anointed king;

18 his enemies will I clothe with shame,
  but on his head shall be a shining crown.'

✶ This important psalm raises many questions. First, as to date, was it composed before or after the exile? Commentators over the past fifty years have argued for a date before the exile, maintaining that the psalm clearly reflects liturgical usage in the time of the monarchy, although opinion differs about what the liturgical background might be. That it was composed after the exile, though probably less likely, cannot be entirely ruled out. Much depends on the inter-

[a] her destitute: *prob. rdg.; Heb.* her provisions.
[b] renew the line of: *lit.* make a horn shoot for.

pretation of verse 17, which arguably may imply that the Davidic succession has been broken, and that its restoration is promised. On such a view, verses 6f. do not reflect actual cultic action, but are a vivid way of recalling the bringing of the Ark to Jerusalem in the time of David. On the other hand, interpretation of the psalm assuming that it was composed before the exile is able to present a plausible liturgical context for such verses. The weaknesses of the former interpretation are the strengths of the latter interpretation, and *vice versa*. A compromise view is that verses 1–16 are a psalm composed before the exile, and verses 17f. an addition made after the exile.

Second, as to liturgical background, if the psalm was composed before the exile, suggestions have included a temple rededication festival, the festival of the enthronement of Yahweh, and the festival of the renewal of the Davidic covenant. In 2 Chron. 6: 41f., verses 8–10 are used in the account of Solomon's dedication of the temple, and this is thus the earliest-known interpretation of at least part of the psalm, whether or not this interpretation is based on any reliable knowledge of the psalm's original setting. Possibly we should envisage a many-sided ceremony which commemorates the dedication of the temple and the establishment of the Davidic covenant (2 Sam. 7: 12), and which reasserts the kingship of the God of Israel. The ceremony may have included a re-enactment of the finding of the Ark, and its bringing to Jerusalem (cp. 2 Sam. 6).

1–5. The speaker is usually held to be the king or a cultic official, but there is no reason why the congregation, the 'we' of verses 6f., should not speak these verses.

1f. *adversity, how he swore:* there is no other record in the historical narratives (e.g. 2 Sam. 7) of either the adversity or the oath, but the treatment of the story may be poetic (cp. Ps. 105) or may rest upon an independent tradition. *Mighty One of Jacob:* cp. Gen. 49: 24. This is an ancient title for God. Its use here may suggest that David recognized that he owed

137

his victories in adversity to the *Mighty One*, and that as Jacob
was the father of the Israelite tribes, so David wished to unite
the tribes in common worship at the 'dwelling' of the
Mighty One of Jacob.

3. *mount my bed*: probably, abstain from marital intercourse, a self-denial that often accompanied vows.

6. *We heard of it*: 'it' is either the Ark of the Covenant or
news about the Ark, or the tradition about David's vow;
but note that 'it' is feminine in the Hebrew, and the Ark is
masculine. A better translation might be 'this'. *Ephrathah . . .
region of Jaar: the region of Jaar* is probably the neighbourhood
of Kiriath-jearim, where the Ark rested for a long period
(1 Sam. 7: 2). *Ephrathah* may either be another name for
Kiriath-jearim, or may be the birth-place of David (Ruth 4:
11).

7. *Let us enter*: in this, and the preceding verse, the congregation either re-enacts the discovery of the Ark and its
arrival in Jerusalem, or enters imaginatively into the recitation
of the story.

8. The Ark, as the symbol of the divine presence, is placed
in its permanent position in the temple. Cp. Num. 10: 35.
This may be a symbolic proclamation of God's kingship (cp.
Ps. 47: 5).

9. This verse perhaps describes the appropriate response of
priest and people to the symbolic placing of the Ark. *righteousness* may be either righteous acts, or garments which symbolize righteousness.

10. It is clear that the anointed king is not David himself,
but a successor.

11–18. These verses are the answer to the prayer of verse
10, spoken probably by a cultic official.

11. *The LORD swore*: this verse balances verse 2. There is
no other record of this oath, but see on verses 1f. With
verses 11f. cp. 2 Sam. 7: 11*b*–16; 1 Kings 8: 25. The verse is
alluded to in Acts 2: 30.

13. *has chosen Zion*: this action was God's initiative, and as

such is an assurance to the people even in the times of disobedience and adversity.

15. The divine grace is directed towards the needy, and the king should also protect the weak and poor.

16. An almost exact repetition of verse 9, except that salvation here, as against 'righteousness' there, expresses the perspective of divine giving.

17. *renew the line:* it is not clear whether the Hebrew has the sense of renew (what has ceased to exist) or of 'maintain'. *light a lamp:* this has been interpreted as 'make a new beginning'. If *lamp* is correct, the perpetually burning sanctuary lamp will be a symbol for the permanence of the Davidic dynasty. In favour of regarding verses 17f. as added after the exile is the fact that verse 17 begins with the word *There* (and contrast 'here' in verse 14*b*), perhaps implying that the writer is not in Jerusalem. For *lamp* cp. 2 Sam. 21: 17, where it may be a royal title.

This psalm expresses more clearly than any other in the Psalter the significance of the Davidic kingship. In contrast to the frequent changes of dynasty in the northern kingdom after the death of Solomon, with the resulting upheaval and bloodshed (1 Kings 15: 25–9; 16: 8–22), the continuance of the Davidic line in the south ensured political stability. Theologically, the Davidic house was, for the people of the south, a symbol of God's favour; it is here acknowledged, however, that this favour was in part conditional upon the obedience of the king to the divine law (verse 12). We can thus understand the fervent wish in this psalm that God will continue to bless the house of David (verse 10). If verses 17f. are a promise added after the exile that God will restore the line of succession that was broken by the exile, the psalm looks forward to a fulfilment in the coming of 'great David's greater son'. ✻

HOW PLEASANT FOR BROTHERS TO LIVE TOGETHER

133

1   How good it is and how pleasant
        for brothers to live[a] together!

2   It is fragrant as oil poured upon the head
        and falling over the beard,
      Aaron's beard, when the oil runs down
        over the collar of his vestments.

3   It is like the dew of Hermon falling
        upon the hills of Zion.
      There the LORD bestows his blessing,
        life for evermore.

✶ The background of this psalm is uncertain. In view of the numerous stories of brothers in conflict in the Old Testament (Cain and Abel, Jacob and Esau, Joseph and his brothers, Absalom and other of the sons of David) it may in fact commend brotherly unity as an ideal, the attainment of which will bring blessing upon Israel. Another view is that it refers to the fellowship experienced when worshippers gathered in Jerusalem for great festivals. The overall interpretation turns on several points of detail.

1. *for brothers to live:* this can be taken literally: the natural rivalry of brothers must be forgotten; or we should render: 'to live together as brothers', in which case, an ideal sort of brotherhood is commended to all. Instead of 'live', it is possible that the verb means 'worship' (N.E.B. footnote). In this sense, it could be used in both interpretations just suggested.

2. The point of the simile is not easy to see. Some interpreters draw attention to the way in which the oil permeates all the clothes of the high priest; similarly, true brotherhood

[a] *Or* to worship.

140

will leaven the lump of Israel. The N.E.B. seems to make the fragrant smell of the oil the point of comparison, while others argue for the refreshing qualities of oil used for anointing. Whether the oil is the sacred oil with which a high priest was anointed, or oil used as a secular cosmetic, is disputed. According to Jewish tradition, high priests were not anointed after the exile. Cp. Ps. 23: 5.

3. *dew of Hermon:* Hermon is the highest mountain in the Lebanon and Anti-Lebanon ranges, which receive the greatest rainfall in the area containing ancient Israel. Perhaps the phrase denotes life-giving and refreshing dew and mist, believed to come from the region of Hermon. *There:* most probably refers to Zion. For this line, see Ps. 128: 5. God's blessing is that his people should enjoy *for evermore* a life of harmony among men and with God. *

BLESS THE LORD

134

Come, bless the LORD,　　　　　　　　　　　1
　　all you servants of the LORD,
who stand night after night
　　in the house of the LORD.
Lift up your hands in the sanctuary　　　　2
　　and bless the LORD.
The LORD, maker of heaven and earth,　　3
　　bless you from Zion!

* This is the last of the 'songs of ascents' (see introduction to Ps. 120). It is not certain that the 'servants of the LORD' (verse 1) are ordinary worshippers as opposed to cultic officials, but if they are then the psalm would be appropriate for a pilgrim festival. The worshippers would be called upon to 'bless the LORD', and in return, a priestly blessing would be pronounced over them (verse 3). A date is impossible to determine.

1. *bless the LORD:* it is not clear whether the servants of the LORD are exhorted to worship God through the medium of set liturgical worship, or to render praise for blessings received from him. The two suggestions are not mutually exclusive, but depend on the identification of the servants. *servants of the LORD:* the N.E.B., by its rendering *night after night* and 'in the sanctuary' (verse 2), implies that cultic officials are meant. In favour of this is the use of *stand*, which often denotes priestly or levitical ministry. On the other hand, 'in the sanctuary' may mean 'towards the sanctuary', envisaging the ordinary worshippers in the temple courts, holding up their hands towards the temple. *night after night:* this has been connected with nightly services at a pilgrim festival, rather than with regular services throughout the year. It is impossible to be dogmatic on this point. For a similar verse, see Ps. 135:1.

3. This may be a priestly blessing pronounced upon pilgrims; cp. Ps. 128: 5. ✻

OUR LORD IS ABOVE ALL GODS

135

1   O praise the LORD.

Praise the name of the LORD;
   praise him, you servants of the LORD,
2 who stand in the house of the LORD,
   in the temple of our God.
3 Praise the LORD, for that is good;*[a]*
   honour his name with psalms, for that is pleasant.
4 The LORD has chosen Jacob to be his own
   and Israel as his special treasure.

[a] *So Pesh.; Heb.* for the LORD is good.

I know that the LORD is great,   5
    that our Lord is above all gods.

Whatever the LORD pleases,   6
    that he does, in heaven and on earth,
    in the sea, in the depths of ocean.

He brings up the mist from the ends of the earth,   7
he opens rifts[a] for the rain,
and brings the wind out of his storehouses.

He struck down all the first-born in Egypt,   8
    both man and beast.

In Egypt[b] he sent signs and portents   9
    against Pharaoh and all his subjects.

He struck down mighty nations   10
    and slew great kings,

Sihon king of the Amorites, Og the king of Bashan,   11
    and all the princes of Canaan,

and gave their land to Israel,   12
    to Israel his people as their patrimony.

O LORD, thy name endures for ever;   13
thy renown, O LORD, shall last for all generations.

The LORD will give his people justice   14
    and have compassion on his servants.

The gods of the nations are idols of silver and gold,   15
    made by the hands of men.

They have mouths that cannot speak   16
    and eyes that cannot see;

they have ears that do not hear,   17
    and there is no breath in their nostrils.[c]

[a] *Prob. rdg.; Heb.* lightnings.
[b] *Lit.* In your midst, Egypt.
[c] *Prob. rdg.; Heb.* mouths.

18   Their makers grow like them,
            and so do all who trust in them.
19   O house of Israel, bless the LORD;
            O house of Aaron, bless the LORD.
20   O house of Levi, bless the LORD;
            you who fear the LORD, bless the LORD.
21   Blessed from Zion be the LORD
            who dwells in Jerusalem.

        O praise the LORD.

✻ The content of this psalm has close parallels with other psalms, and passages from the Pentateuch. The most striking parallels are verses 15–18 and Ps. 115: 4–8, and verses 10–12 and Ps. 136: 17–22; yet the psalm has an integrity of its own. It begins with a call to the 'servants of the LORD' (who are presumably the same as those addressed in verses 19f.) to praise God, and ends with a call to bless him. In between, the psalmist asserts God's lordship both in nature (verses 6–9) and in history (verses 8–12), the former shading into the latter. This lordship is then contrasted with that of the other gods, who have no more power than the men who make their images (verses 15–18). Some interpreters connect the psalm with the celebration of Passover, because there is no mention of the Sinai covenant, and because it is widely held that the Sinai covenant was commemorated at the Feast of Tabernacles. However, such suggestions probably assume knowledge that outruns the evidence available.

    1. *O praise the LORD:* see on Ps. 106: 1, and cp. verse 21. *praise* will include recalling his mighty acts in nature and history, so that at the end of the psalm, God can be blessed for his works. *servants of the LORD:* see on Ps. 134: 1.

    2. *temple courts:* if the servants are all those mentioned in verses 19f., the ordinary worshippers would be those who

stood in the courts, although some interpreters prefer to see the reference to ministers alone.

3. The N.E.B. rendering provides a good parallelism.

4. The choice of Israel was made especially at the exodus.

5f. These verses form the introduction to the rehearsal of God's works in nature (verses 7–9) and in history (verses 8–12). The speaker of these verses (*I know . . .*) may be an individual leader of the congregation. *above all gods:* in this psalm, these words must be interpreted in the light of verses 15–18. Verse 6 states that God's will is operative in the whole of the created world.

7. For this verse, see Jer. 10: 13; 51: 16. *he opens rifts:* the N.E.B. *bedāqim* (rifts) for Hebrew *berāqim* (lightning) compares a phrase in an ancient Canaanite text (*Ancient Near Eastern Texts*, p. 135), 'I'll open rifts in the clouds.' The Hebrew is literally 'he made (makes) lightnings for rain' and if correct, it is best explained on the view that lightning often accompanies heavy rain in the Near East.

8–12. This hymnic summary of the chief events of the exodus and conquest does not try to be fully comprehensive and shows a poetic use of history (cp. Ps. 105). Ps. 136: 10–22 repeats and expands the material. For Pharaoh, see Exod. 7–11. For the Israelite defeats of Sihon and Og, cp. Num. 21: 21–6, 33–5.

13f. The psalmist affirms that God's character revealed in the exodus, as one who acts to deliver the oppressed, is an unchanging character on which his people will be ever able to rely. This is not so of the gods mentioned in the following verses.

15–18. See Ps. 115: 4–8.

19f. See Pss. 115: 9–11; 118: 2–4.

21. *Blessed from Zion:* probably 'May the Lord be blessed by those who gather in Zion to worship him.' ✳

136

1   It is good to give thanks to the LORD,
        for his love endures for ever.

2   Give thanks to the God of gods;
        his love endures for ever.

3   Give thanks to the Lord of lords;
        his love endures for ever.

4   Alone he works great marvels;
        his love endures for ever.

5   In wisdom he made the heavens;
        his love endures for ever.

6   He laid the earth upon the waters;
        his love endures for ever.

7   He made the great lights,
        his love endures for ever,

8   the sun to rule by day,
        his love endures for ever,

9   the moon and the stars to rule by night;
        his love endures for ever.

10   He struck down the first-born of the Egyptians,
        his love endures for ever,

11   and brought Israel from among them;
        his love endures for ever.

12   With strong hand and outstretched arm,
        his love endures for ever,

13   he divided the Red Sea in two,
        his love endures for ever,

14   and made Israel pass through it,
        his love endures for ever;

but Pharaoh and his host he swept into the sea;   15
    his love endures for ever.

He led his people through the wilderness;   16
    his love endures for ever.

He struck down great kings;   17
    his love endures for ever.

He slew mighty kings,   18
    his love endures for ever,

Sihon king of the Amorites,   19
    his love endures for ever,

and Og the king of Bashan;   20
    his love endures for ever.

He gave their land to Israel,   21
    his love endures for ever,

to Israel his servant as their patrimony;   22
    his love endures for ever.

He remembered us when we were cast down,   23
    his love endures for ever,

and rescued us from our enemies;   24
    his love endures for ever.

He gives food to all his creatures;   25
    his love endures for ever.

Give thanks to the God of heaven,   26
    for his love endures for ever.

✼ The repeated refrain of this psalm suggests that it was used antiphonally, though we cannot be certain about the disposition of the choirs (or, perhaps, soloists). After the preliminary giving of thanks (verses 1–3), the psalm deals with God's works in creation (verses 4–9), the exodus (verses 10–16), and the wilderness wanderings and conquest of Canaan (verses 17–22). Verses 23f. remember further occasions of divine deliverance, and verse 25 praises God for his bounty in providing food for all creatures. Verse 25 strikes the modern reader as odd in its context. Some interpreters regard it as a later gloss, while another view is that the psalm was a harvest thanksgiving psalm, and that verse 25 is the climax. If verse 25 is rightly interpreted as referring to all living things, then the overall structure of the psalm is that it begins with the universality of God, and then concentrates on his particular revelation to Israel, before returning to a general statement about his universal providence. Verses 10–22 closely parallel Ps. 135: 9–12, though it is impossible to say what is the literary connection between the passages, if any.

1. *It is good:* see on Ps. 106: 1.

2f. *God of gods . . . Lord of lords:* cp. Deut. 10: 17 and Ps. 135: 5. The two phrases express the absolute sovereignty of God.

4. *great marvels:* these include God's works both in nature and history.

5–9. The works of creation. This section has similarities with Gen. 1: 16f. (verses 7–9) and with 'wisdom' traditions of creation, e.g. Prov. 3: 19 (cp. verse 5), but it seems to be a unique blend of these traditions. In verse 6, *laid upon* uses a word which denotes the beating of metal into a thin sheet. The passage implies that the wisdom by which God made the created order can be discerned indirectly by man, as he ponders the creation (cp. Ps. 8).

10–15. The exodus. Again, the section has affinities with other traditions, but is in itself unique. The rare verb *swept* (verse 15, literally 'shook off') occurs at Exod. 14: 27, while the verb *divided* (verse 13) is used of the parting of the Red Sea only in this psalm.

16–22. Compare Ps. 135: 10–12 (note that at 135: 12 it is 'Israel his people') and Deut. 2: 26 – 3: 7.

23f. Although some interpreters specify a particular time of divine rescue (e.g. the period of the Judges or the exile in Babylon) it is hazardous to seek to be so precise.

25. *to all his creatures:* literally 'to all flesh', probably all living things. ✲

IF I FORGET YOU, O JERUSALEM

137

By the rivers of Babylon we sat down and wept   1
  when we remembered Zion.
There on the willow-trees*ᵃ*   2
  we hung up our harps,
for there those who carried us off   3
  demanded music and singing,
and our captors called on us to be merry:
  'Sing us one of the songs of Zion.'
How could we sing the LORD's song   4
  in a foreign land?

If I forget you, O Jerusalem,   5
  let my right hand wither away;
let my tongue cling to the roof of my mouth   6
  if I do not remember you,
if I do not set Jerusalem
  above my highest joy.
Remember, O LORD, against the people of Edom   7
  the day of Jerusalem's fall,
when they said, 'Down with it, down with it,
  down to its very foundations!'
O Babylon, Babylon*ᵇ* the destroyer,   8
  happy the man who repays you
  for all that you did to us!

[a] *Or* poplars.
[b] O Babylon, Babylon: *lit.* O daughter of Babylon.

Happy is he who shall seize your children
and dash them against the rock.

* This psalm is clearly related to the Babylonian exile, although its exact date and purpose of composition are a matter
for discussion. Many commentators maintain that the tenses
of verses 1–3 indicate that the psalm was written after the
return from exile, but while Babylon was still sufficiently
prosperous for verses 8f. to be appropriate. A date, say, between 540 and 520 is thus suggested. Some interpreters go
further, and say that verses 1–4, and or verse 7, imply that the
psalmist witnessed the destruction of the temple, and was
himself involved in the events described in verses 1–3. Although this is not impossible (the psalmist, in this case, would
most reasonably be in his seventies), it begs the question of
the purpose of the psalm. A strong case can be made for the
view that the psalm is primarily a curse against Babylon,
and that God is exhorted to remember Israel's enemies
(verse 7), because Israel did not fail to remember Jerusalem
(verses 5f.). On this view, the 'we' of verses 1–4 is the 'we'
of the whole people identifying themselves with their fathers;
it is not necessary to suppose that the psalmist himself had
been in Babylon. Another approach is to regard the psalm as
based upon a lamentation during the exile, with the curse
being part of the lamentation (cp. Lam. 1: 20–2). Attractive
as this view is, it cannot be proved or disproved.

It is probably best to accept that the questions of date and purpose are more open than is commonly supposed. The real problem for the modern reader is the vindictive nature of verses 8f.
There is no point in trying to deny that the verses are
vindictive; they must be seen, however, in the context of the
Israelite belief in God's justice, and in Jerusalem as the dwelling
place of God. The Israelites could not conceive that a nation
that had lifted up its hand to destroy God's sanctuary would
escape punishment; they had yet to learn that God's ways are

not man's ways, and that suffering love can reconcile former enemies.

1. *rivers of Babylon:* this would include the many canals as well as the main rivers and their tributaries. *sat down . . . when we remembered:* some see a technical use of the verb, meaning 'to worship' (cp. Ps. 133: 1, N.E.B. footnote). The verse could refer to either organized worship, or spontaneous grief.

2. *we hung up:* presumably as a sign of distress, and as an answer to the tormenters of verse 3.

3. Possibly the torment was that the exiles were ordered to sing hymns celebrating the impregnability of Zion, such as Ps. 46.

4. *How could we sing:* there is no suggestion here that the songs cannot be sung, because God is confined to his own land. Such a view would go against all that is expressed, for example, in Ps. 135. Rather, a song of Zion would be quite inappropriate in a foreign land, which symbolized that God's people stood under such judgement that God had allowed his sanctuary to be destroyed.

5f. The unfailing loyalty to Jerusalem is expressed in the form of two oaths. *forget you:* the N.E.B. translation, although probably correct, does not convey the Hebrew word-play as does the rendering 'If I forget you . . . let my right hand forget (her cunning).'

7. A curse against Edom – the deeds of Edom at the time of the exile are bitterly recalled at Obad. verses 8–14 (cp. Lam. 4: 21f.).

8. *Babylon the destroyer:* against the N.E.B., the traditional Hebrew text is literally 'who are destroyed' or 'are to be destroyed'. The fact that Babylon was not destroyed, at any rate at its capture by Cyrus, king of Persia in 540 B.C., makes this interpretation the more difficult and, therefore, the more likely interpretation.

9. The practice here described was apparently a feature of warfare. ✲

LET ALL THE KINGS OF THE EARTH PRAISE THEE,
O LORD

138

1 I will praise thee, O LORD,*a* with all my heart;
boldly, O God, will I sing psalms to thee.*b*
2 I will bow down towards thy holy temple,
for thy love and faithfulness I will praise thy name;
for thou hast made thy promise wide as the heavens.
3 When I called to thee thou didst answer me
and make me bold and valiant-hearted.
4 Let all the kings of the earth praise*c* thee, O LORD,
when they hear the words thou hast spoken;
5 and let them sing of*d* the LORD's ways,
for great is the glory of the LORD.
6 For the LORD, high as he is, cares for the lowly,
and from afar he humbles the proud.
7 Though I walk among foes thou dost preserve my life,
exerting thy power against the rage of my enemies,
and with thy right hand thou savest me.
8 The LORD will accomplish his purpose for me.
Thy true love, O LORD, endures for ever;
leave not thy work unfinished.

✻ The date and original setting of this psalm depend on the
interpretation of verse 1. If we translate verse 1*b* as in the
N.E.B. footnote, 'I will sing psalms to thee before the gods',
the identity of the gods must be determined. If they have real
power, but power inferior to that of the God of Israel, the

[*a*] O LORD: *so some MSS.; others om.*
[*b*] boldly . . . thee: *or* I will sing psalms to thee before the gods.
[*c*] *Or* confess.
[*d*] *Or* walk in.

psalm may well be an ancient composition. If, however, as in Isa. 40–55, the gods are adjudged to be powerless, and are summoned to witness the mighty deeds of the God of Israel, then the psalm may have been composed after the exile, and is perhaps a thanksgiving for deliverance from the exile. Those who feel that only a king could have spoken verse 4, take the composition to be a royal psalm. Although the original date and setting can hardly now be determined, the psalm is a noble expression, in only a few verses, of thanksgiving for God's greatness (verses 4f.), his promises (verses 2 and 7), his concern for the weak (verse 6) and the sure triumph of his purposes (verse 8).

1. *boldly, O God:* however we identify the gods here (N.E.B. footnote) the verse is a confident expression of the psalmist's loyalty.

2. *I will bow down:* literally 'I will prostrate myself'. *towards thy holy temple:* in the direction of the temple, the symbol of God's presence. *promise wide as the heavens:* for *promise* cp. Ps. 119: 11, and see p. 92. The N.E.B. *heavens* is a probable conjecture for the awkward Hebrew 'thou hast made the promise greater than all thy name'.

3. The tenses could also be present, expressing constant truths; see verse 7.

4. *words thou hast spoken:* probably, God's promises to Israel, and his purposes through Israel for the whole world.

6. *lowly:* refers more to an external condition than an internal state of mind. *humbles the proud:* the N.E.B. assumes that we have here not the common verb 'to know', but another verb of the same form meaning 'to humble'. The case is difficult to decide, and both make good sense. If we accept 'knows the proud', then the verse expresses the immanence and transcendence of God who, *high as he is*, has intimate knowledge of the thoughts of the proud. Cp. Ps. 82: 3f.

7. The foes and troubles cannot be identified; this verse echoes verse 3.

8. The psalm closes with an affirmation that God's purpose for the psalmist will be fulfilled, which turns into a prayer that his wider purposes for Israel, and perhaps the world, will triumph. ✻

WHERE CAN I FLEE FROM THY PRESENCE?

139

1 LORD, thou hast examined me and knowest me.
2 Thou knowest all, whether I sit down or rise up;
    thou hast discerned my thoughts from afar.
3 Thou hast traced my journey and my resting places,
    and art familiar with all my paths.
4 For there is not a word on my tongue
    but thou, LORD, knowest them all.[a]
5 Thou hast kept close guard before me and behind
    and hast spread thy hand over me.
6 Such knowledge is beyond my understanding,
    so high that I cannot reach it.
7 Where can I escape from thy spirit?
    Where can I flee from thy presence!
8 If I climb up to heaven, thou art there;
    if I make my bed in Sheol, again I find thee.
9 If I take my flight to the frontiers of the morning
    or dwell at the limit of the western sea,
10 even there thy hand will meet me
    and thy right hand will hold me fast.
11 If I say, 'Surely darkness will steal over me,
    night will close around me',[b]

[a] For . . . them all: *or* If there is any offence on my tongue, thou, LORD, knowest it all.
[b] night . . . me: *so Scroll; Heb.* and the day around me turn to night.

darkness is no darkness for thee 12
  and night is luminous as day;
   to thee both dark and light are one.

Thou it was who didst fashion my inward parts; 13
thou didst knit me together in my mother's womb.
I will praise thee, for thou dost fill me with awe; 14
wonderful thou art,*a* and wonderful thy works.
Thou knowest me through and through:
  my body is no mystery to thee, 15
how I was secretly kneaded into shape
  and patterned in the depths of the earth.
Thou didst see my limbs unformed in the womb, 16
  and in thy book they are all recorded;
   day by day they were fashioned,
   not one of them was late in growing.*b*

How deep I find thy thoughts, O God, 17
  how inexhaustible their themes!

Can I count them? They outnumber the grains of sand; 18
to finish the count, my years must equal thine.

O God, if only thou wouldst slay the wicked! 19
If those men of blood would but leave me in peace—
those who provoke thee*c* with deliberate evil 20
  and rise*d* in vicious rebellion against thee!
How I hate them, O Lord, that hate thee! 21
I am cut to the quick when they oppose thee;
I hate them with undying hatred; 22
  I hold them all my enemies.

[a] *So Sept.; Heb.* I am.
[b] was late in growing: *prob. rdg.; Heb. om.*
[c] *So one form of Sept.; Heb.* speak of thee.
[d] rise: *so Scroll; Heb. obscure.*

23 Examine me, O God, and know my thoughts;
     test me, and understand my misgivings.
24 Watch lest I follow any path that grieves thee;
     guide me in the ancient*a* ways.

✻ Interpreters have been much exercised in their attempts to
classify this psalm according to the psalm types, and to dis-
cover its original setting and purpose; yet it is questionable
whether any such attempts shed light on a text that is largely
self-explanatory. The main problem for the interpreter is to
account for verses 19–22. An older view was that the psalm
raised the problem of evil by asking, in effect, how the all-
seeing, all-knowing and ever-present God could tolerate
wicked men. However, this view rather forces the meaning
of verses 19–22. A more recent solution has proposed that the
psalmist had been accused of unfaithfulness to God by the
enemies mentioned in verses 19–22, and that the psalm is in
some way connected with his ordeal before God, designed to
test his innocence. If this latter solution were correct, it
would enrich our knowledge of ancient Israelite practice,
but of itself, it hardly adds anything to the theological understanding of the psalm. It seems best to let the text speak for
itself.

Verses 1–6 describe God's intimate knowledge of the psalmist's thoughts and ways, leading into an affirmation that no-
where can the psalmist flee from God's presence (verses 7–12);
verses 13–18 meditate on the divine overseeing of human
creation. In verses 19–22, the psalmist reacts violently against
his enemies, who are also God's enemies; loyalty to God will
entail hostility to such men. Finally, there is a prayer (verses
23f.) that the God who knows the psalmist so intimately,
will actively guide him according to the divine will.

1. *thou hast examined me:* according to the 'ordeal' theory,
the past tenses indicate that the ordeal is over, and that the

[*a*] *Or* everlasting.

psalmist is now giving thanks for his deliverance. The verse is best understood, however, as a general statement which is elaborated in verses 2–5.

2. *sit down or rise up:* a Hebrew way of saying 'whatever I do in every aspect of my life'; and cp. the expressions in verse 3. *from afar:* either cp. Ps. 138: 6*b*, or translate 'beforehand'. This latter interpretation does not deny free choice to the psalmist.

3. *Thou hast traced:* in the sense of measured out beforehand. Another possible rendering is 'examined' (literally 'sifted, winnowed').

4. The N.E.B. footnote may allow for the 'ordeal' theory.

5. God's knowledge of the psalmist also involves practical guidance and protection.

7–12. God is omnipresent.

7. *spirit* and *presence* are terms by which the psalmist speaks of the reality of God in the world of men; yet this reality remains essentially a mystery beyond human understanding (see verse 6). The questions do not mean that the psalmist wishes to escape from God!

8. The statement that God is present in Sheol contradicts other statements in the psalms (e.g. Ps. 88: 5) that those in Sheol are cut off from God's help. It may be that the psalmist is using a type of expression found elsewhere in the Old Testament (e.g. Amos 9: 2) and the ancient Near East. But we must not expect all statements in the psalms to be consistent with each other; and to deny that this verse affirms that God is present in Sheol is to detract from what the whole section says about God's unbounded presence.

9. *frontiers of the morning . . . sea:* poetic expressions for furthest east and west.

10. *meet me:* the traditional rendering 'lead me' is also possible.

11f. *darkness is no darkness:* even darkness, which held terrors for ancient as for modern man, does not bring about an absence of God.

13. *inward parts:* literally 'kidneys', usually a term for man's emotional life. The two lines of this verse probably denote the whole person, physical and emotional. The psalm asserts that God's work of creation is never finished, but that he is involved in all new creative processes. This thought clearly raises the problem of evil, but it does not warrant forced interpretations of verses 19–22.

14. The N.E.B. footnote implies a number of slight alterations to the Hebrew. For traditional renderings see, for example, the Authorized Version: 'I will praise thee; for I am fearfully and wonderfully made: marvellous are thy works; and that my soul knoweth right well.'

15. *kneaded into shape:* the language may be influenced by, but not necessarily expressive of, stories about man's creation circulating widely in the ancient Near East. In these stories, the gods created man by fashioning him from clay (and cp. Gen. 2: 7). Similar stories are found in many folk beliefs throughout the world.

16. This is a difficult verse, and some translations have 'my deeds' instead of *my limbs*, and, 'the days that were formed for me' (so the Revised Standard Version) for *day by day they were fashioned*. These alternatives affect the interpretation. The N.E.B. implies that the ordered development of the embryo into a person was recorded in God's book. The other translations suggest that the whole course of the psalmist's life was mapped out before birth.

18. *to finish the count:* the N.E.B. is a free paraphrase of 'were I to reach the end I would still be with thee'.

19–22. The psalmist speaks of a tension known to all God-fearing people, between the knowledge of a gracious and almighty God and the fact of having to live with wicked and godless people. The psalmist cannot be loyal to both; he takes his stand on the side of God, and this inevitably leads to mutual hostility between the psalmist and his enemies. Verse 20 is a very difficult verse in the Hebrew, and N.E.B. can be accepted as a likely way of solving its problems.

23f. The 'ordeal' theory sees in *Examine me* a plea for God's judgement in the ordeal; further, the word for *grieves* (verse 24) is connected with a word for 'idol', and it is suggested that the psalmist had been accused of idolatry. The translation 'idolatry' could be accepted, without also implying acceptance of the 'ordeal' theory. *the ancient ways:* or: 'everlasting ways' (N.E.B. footnote), the paths chosen by God, which lead to life. As in Ps. 138, the psalm ends with a prayer for what has previously been affirmed; for such prayer ultimately denotes that dependence upon God which is the heart of true religion. ✳

THE LORD WILL GIVE THEIR DUE TO THE NEEDY

140

Rescue me, O LORD, from evil men;   1
   keep me safe from violent men,
whose heads are full of wicked schemes,   2
   who stir up contention day after day.
Their tongues are sharp as serpents' fangs;   3
   on their lips is spiders'[a] poison.
Guard me, O LORD, from wicked men;   4
   keep me safe from violent men.
   who plan to thrust me out of the way.
Arrogant men set hidden traps for me,   5
   rogues spread their nets
   and lay snares for me along the path.
I said, 'O LORD, thou art my God;   6
   O LORD, hear my plea for mercy.
O LORD God, stronghold of my safety,   7
thou hast shielded my head in the day of battle.

[a] *Mng. of Heb. word uncertain.*

8–9 Frustrate, O LORD, their designs against me;
never let the wicked gain their purpose.
If any of those at my table rise against me,
let their own conspiracies be their undoing.
10 Let burning coals be tipped upon them;
let them be plunged into the miry depths,
never to rise again.
11 Slander shall find no home in the land;
evil and violence shall be hounded to destruction.'

12 I know that the LORD will give their due to the needy
and justice to the downtrodden.
13 Righteous men will surely give thanks to thy name;
the upright will worship in thy presence.

☆ This psalm begins with a plea that God will deliver the psalmist from wicked and violent men who are his enemies (verses 1–5). In verses 6–11, the psalmist declares that he has always been loyal to God, and that he rejected any part in conspiracies. The psalm closes with a confident affirmation that God will uphold justice, and deliver the needy (verses 12f.). The identification of the psalmist and his enemies is impossible. Some say that the palmist is a king or commander, because of verse 7, in which case the enemies may be foreign armies. Against this, it is asserted that the language of verse 7 has been taken from royal psalms. It is probably best merely to note that, as in other similar psalms, the reality of evil in the world is faced with the conviction that God's ways are, and will be, vindicated. A date cannot be determined.

1f. We have no clue about the identity of the *evil men* or their *wicked schemes*. The word translated *contention* is literally 'wars', but if the enemies are men within Israel, then the N.E.B.'s 'contention' is a good rendering.

3. The slanderous rumour-spreading of the enemies is vividly described.

4f. The request of verse 1 is repeated, but the idea of thrusting the psalmist out of his *way* (literally 'steps') leads on to metaphors in which the enemies are described as hunters seeking their prey.

6. *I said:* the psalmist appears to recall previous declarations of loyalty, unless the phrase is to be translated 'I say'.

7. *day of battle:* literally 'weapons'. The language may be figurative, as in verse 5.

8f. The Hebrew is very difficult, and the N.E.B. has re-distributed the words between the two verses. *those at my table* would imply that members of the psalmist's household or circle of friends were among his enemies; but the N.E.B. is a free rendering of the Hebrew 'those who surround me', which could also have a hostile sense.

10. The background to this verse may be the incident of Sodom and Gomorrah, when those cities were overthrown by fire from heaven (Gen. 19: 24f.) and the swallowing by the earth of Korah, Dathan and Abiram (Num. 16: 12–35). The translation *miry depths* assumes that the Hebrew word, which occurs only here, is the same as one found in ancient Canaan-ite literature meaning 'pit'.

11. *Slander . . . evil and violence:* literally 'the slanderer . . . the evil and violent man'. *hounded:* there is, perhaps, a re-miniscence of the hounding which the evil men did, according to verse 5.

12f. The concluding affirmation. *worship in thy presence* may be too narrow, in spite of the parallelism, and the tradi-tional 'dwell' is to be preferred. The dwelling in security in God's land will, of course, include the privilege of worship. ✷

I WOULD RATHER BE BUFFETED BY
THE RIGHTEOUS

141

O Lord, I call to thee, come quickly to my aid;   1
    listen to my cry when I call to thee.

2   Let my prayer be like incense duly set before thee
      and my raised hands like the evening sacrifice.

3   Set a guard, O LORD, over my mouth;
      keep watch at the door of my lips.

4   Turn not my heart to sinful thoughts
      nor to any pursuit of evil courses.
    The evildoers appal me;[a]
      not for me the delights of their table.

5   I would rather be buffeted by the righteous
      and reproved by good men.
  My head shall not be anointed with the oil of wicked
          men,
    for that would make me a party to their crimes.

6   They shall founder on the rock of justice
      and shall learn how acceptable my words are.

7 Their bones shall be scattered at the mouth of Sheol,
    like splinters of wood or stone on the ground.

8   But my eyes are fixed on thee, O LORD God;
      thou art my refuge; leave me not unprotected.

9 Keep me from the trap which they have set for me,
    from the snares of evildoers.

10   Let the wicked fall into their own nets,
     whilst I pass in safety, all alone.

✻ The psalmist prays for deliverance at a time when he is threatened by evildoers (verse 9). He asserts that he has strenuously avoided the company of the evildoers (verses 4b–5), yet he acknowledges that this does not make him righteous. Only the strength and grace that come from God (verses 3–4a) can do that. Verses 6 and 7 are notoriously difficult to translate. If we follow the N.E.B. at verse 7, the

[a] appal me: *prob. rdg.; Heb.* with men.

psalmist confidently looks forward to the confounding of his enemies. The more traditional text of verse 7, however, is 'Our bones are scattered . . .', which makes verse 7 the beginning of the final plea for help. Although the nature of the psalmist's plight cannot be determined, the psalm speaks of confident trust in God in the face of adversity, on the part of one whose whole life is directed towards God. The psalm was probably composed after the exile.

2. *be like incense . . . like the evening sacrifice:* it is not possible to be certain whether this refers to actual 'incense' or the smoke of the burnt offering, whether it refers to a morning or evening offering, or whether the psalmist was away from Jerusalem or in some way prevented from making a sacrificial offering. However, it is clear that he associates his prayer in some way with the regular offerings of the Jerusalem temple.

3. *Set a guard:* although it is from the heart that a man speaks, and thus the heart (in the sense of a man's deepest thoughts and desires) needs to be directed aright, care in what is spoken can also strengthen the good in a person. The psalmist acknowledges his need for divine aid in this.

4. *Turn not my heart:* do not fail to help me, otherwise I may pursue *evil courses. The evildoers appal me:* Hebrew 'in company with men who are evildoers', which follows on closely from the previous line. *delights of their table:* Hebrew 'dainties'. This may suggest either sharing food with them (a sign of fellowship and agreement), or imitating their way of life. It may be right to infer from 'dainties' that the evildoers are rich, and live affluent lives.

5. *buffeted:* although the Hebrew word has the sense of hitting physically, it may here be figurative of stern and harsh reproof. *My head shall not . . . a party to their crimes:* Hebrew 'Let not my head refuse anointing oil, for my prayer will continue against their wicked deeds' (though this is only one possible translation). The N.E.B. continues the thought of verses 4*b*–5*a*. If the traditional Hebrew text is correct, the

anointing oil may symbolize the reproof of *the righteous*. Against the N.E.B., it is probable that the conclusion of the phrase does contain the idea of praying that the crimes of the psalmist's enemies will be punished.

6. *They shall founder . . .:* Hebrew 'Their judges shall be cast down by the sides of the rock' possibly meaning that the judges who acquit the guilty evildoers will not escape punishment. The N.E.B. partly paraphrases this idea. *learn how acceptable:* some vindication of the psalmist is envisaged.

7. *Their bones . . . Sheol:* the N.E.B. transposes the lines of the Hebrew. The imagery is that of the sort of scattered fragments that are left at the site where a woodcutter or stonemason has been at work. With this is combined the image of the bones of dismembered bodies, possibly killed in war. Had the bodies been properly buried, the persons would have entered Sheol. As it is, the bones are *scattered at the mouth of Sheol*, perhaps denying to the dead even shadowy existence in Sheol. Non-burial would be regarded as a dreadful fate (and cp. Ps. 79: 2). The N.E.B. sees the evildoers as the victims. A stronger attested tradition, as well as the more difficult reading, is 'our bones', i.e. the psalmist and perhaps his righteous friends. In this case, the metaphor is a strong expression of the psalmist's distress, and his confident trust is all the more remarkable.

10. *all alone:* this is a possible rendering of a difficult word, which it is difficult to relate to the psalm as a whole. 'At the same time' is another possibility.

The whole psalm asserts that true religion is a fellowship with God that withstands all adversity; it prefers the correction that will deepen such fellowship, to the superficial attractions of compromise and luxury. ✽

SAVE ME...SET ME FREE

142

I cry aloud to the Lord;   1
  to the Lord I plead aloud for mercy.
I pour out my complaint before him   2
and tell over my troubles in his presence.
When my spirit is faint within me,   3
  thou art there to watch over my steps.
In the path that I should take
  they have hidden a snare.
I look to my right hand,   4
  I find no friend by my side;
no way of escape is in sight,
  no one comes to rescue me.
I cry to thee, O Lord,   5
  and say, 'Thou art my refuge;
thou art all I have*a*
  in the land of the living.
Give me a hearing when I cry,   6
  for I am brought very low;
save me from my pursuers,
  for they are too strong for me.
Set me free from my prison,   7
  so that I may praise thy name.'
The righteous shall crown me with garlands,*b*
  when thou givest me my due reward.

✶ This short psalm is a passionate plea for help in the face
of some sort of persecution. The psalmist feels so totally

[*a*] all I have: *lit.* my portion.
[*b*] crown me with garlands: *or* crowd round me.

alone that he expects no help from any friend (verse 4). His enemies are too strong for him (verse 6), but in his weakness he finds strength from God (verse 3) and he looks forward to rejoicing in company with those loyal to God. The meaning of verse 7a is not clear, and may refer either to actual imprisonment, or may be a figurative description for emotional and spiritual distress. Again, it is not clear that 'Thou art my refuge' in verse 5 shows that the psalmist had sought sanctuary in the temple, and awaited a legal decision about his future. This is a possible, rather than probable, line of interpretation. A date is impossible to determine.

1. *I cry aloud:* not only because of the intensity of the distress, but because it was probably customary for private prayer to be audible.

2. *in his presence:* possibly, but not necessarily, in the sanctuary.

3. *thou art there:* Hebrew 'thou it is who knowest my path'. The N.E.B. perhaps tries to bring out the force of 'knowest', with a paraphrase.

4. *I look . . . I find:* another reading is 'Look on the right and see that (or for) there is no friend . . .' This would make the psalmist's appeal to God even more urgent. The *right hand* is the place from which help could be expected.

5. *all I have in the land of the living:* the *land of the living* is in contrast to the underworld; yet life is at best a matter of quality, and the psalmist seeks not merely the avoidance of death, but the privilege of life in which the service of God is his most treasured thing.

7. *Set me free . . .:* Hebrew 'bring my soul out of prison'. Although 'soul' (Hebrew *nephesh*) can denote the whole person, in the present phrase it may denote the emotional and spiritual life of the psalmist, which is figuratively in prison. *crown me with garlands:* it is not possible to reconstruct the nature of the psalmist's misfortunes, nor the nature of his victorious reception by the righteous, except that restoration to full fellowship and worship seems to be implied. For anci-

ent Jewish interpretation, the mention of 'crowning' suggested the triumph of David after his troubles at the hand of
Saul, and the title of the psalm was connected with David
taking refuge in the cave (1 Sam. 24: 3) during his flight from
Saul. ✻

ATHIRST FOR GOD

143

LORD, hear my prayer;   1
be true to thyself, and listen to my pleading;
   then in thy righteousness answer me.
Bring not thy servant to trial before thee;   2
against thee no man on earth can be right.
An enemy has hunted me down,   3
   has ground my living body under foot
and plunged me into darkness like a man long dead,
so that my spirit fails me   4
   and my heart is dazed with despair.
I dwell upon the years long past,   5
   upon the memory of all that thou hast done;
   the wonders of thy creation fill my mind.
To thee I lift my outspread hands,   6
   athirst for thee in a thirsty land.
LORD, make haste to answer,   7
   for my spirit faints.
Do not hide thy face from me
or I shall be like those who go down to the abyss.
In the morning let me know thy true love;   8
   I have put my trust in thee.
Show me the way that I must take;
   to thee I offer all my heart.

9 Deliver me, LORD, from my enemies,
     for with thee have I sought refuge.*a*

10 Teach me to do thy will, for thou art my God;
     in thy gracious kindness, show me the level road.*b*

11 Keep me safe, O LORD, for the honour of thy name
     and, as thou art just, release me from my distress.

12 In thy love for me, reduce my enemies to silence
     and bring destruction on all who oppress me;
          for I am thy servant.

✱ This is the prayer of a man who has been brought very
low before his enemies (verses 3f.) and whose suffering is made
unbearable by his sense of dereliction (verse 7). Recalling
God's faithfulness and his past acts of salvation (verses 1, 5),
he comes longing for his presence (verses 6–8) and pleading
for deliverance (verses 9–12). His plea is for mercy rather
than for justice, because he is all too well aware of his own
unworthiness (verse 2) and his need for a closer walk with
God (verses 8, 10). Hence this has become one of the Penitential Psalms in Christian tradition, the last of the seven in the
Psalter. Originally it may have been used in night vigils,
for it is one of several that looks for God's help to come in the
morning (verse 8; see p. 14, sect. C).

1 f. He appeals for mercy, trusting himself to God's faithfulness.

1. *be true to thyself*: literally 'in thy faithfulness'. God's
righteousness is seen in his faithfulness to his promise to protect his loyal servants, it is the revealed demonstration of his
trustworthiness in the lives of his saints. The answer the psalmist seeks in no mere verbal response, but a further demonstration of God's favour in his own life.

2. It is sometimes held on the basis of this verse that the

[a] with . . . refuge: *so one MS.; others* unto thee have I hidden.
[b] road: *so many MSS.; others* land.

168

psalm was written for the use of an accused man on the eve of his trial, but since the psalmist offers no protestation of innocence, this seems an unlikely interpretation (cp. on 5: 3; 17: 1). Indeed, he makes no reference to any accusation by his enemies; his total concern here is with his standing before God, and he knows that no man can be found blameless if examined against God's perfection. The psalm is remarkable in implying that man's acceptance by God is based on God's grace, and not on his own righteousness.

3f. He is brought so low that he already is as good as dead and buried.

3. *An enemy:* a collective noun; cp. the plural in verse 9. In other vigil psalms the enemies are often portrayed as nightmarish creatures, suggesting identification with the demonic powers of darkness (cp. 57: 4; 59: 6f.). Here it is rather the suffering they have inflicted on the psalmist that has the nightmarish quality. *ground my living body:* literally 'crushed my life to the earth', that is into the grave. *into darkness:* probably the darkness of death or Sheol (cp. 88: 12). The language of this verse is, of course, figurative of very severe distress, but it speaks also of the absence of God, for his presence means life and peace (note the contrast between death and God's presence in verse 7).

5–8. Remembering God's former blessings, he pleads for help to come soon, 'In the morning'.

5. *all that thou hast done:* in the history of Israel, but also in the lives of individuals.

6. *I lift my outspread hands:* a traditional attitude of both prayer (28: 2) and praise (134: 2). *athirst for thee in a thirsty land:* a metaphor of longing for God's nearness similar to those in 42: 1 and 63: 1. Thirst and water are common symbols of spiritual longing and satisfaction in both Testaments (e.g. Isa. 55: 1; Rev. 21: 6).

7. *my spirit faints:* I have no strength left, my vitality drains away. Hence the comparison with *those who go down to the abyss*, that is the dead (cp. 28: 1). *Do not hide thy face:* a prayer

that God will look again in blessing and so restore the life-giving knowledge of his presence (contrast Num. 6: 25). See also on verse 3 above.

8. *In the morning:* the rising sun that brings warmth and light to earth thus dispelling the distress and darkness of night is an apt symbol of God's healing presence (cp. Mal. 4: 2). *thy true love:* seen in God's faithfulness to his promise to protect and bless his servants (cp. verse 1). *the way:* the path of healing, life and joy (119: 25–32), but also the way of righteousness and obedience to God (1: 6). It is therefore a road that can only be walked in trust and with a total commitment of the heart.

9–12. Having dedicated his life to God, he calls again for release, guidance and healing.

10. *Teach me to do thy will:* the parallelism indicates that this expression is synonymous with *show me the level road* (see on verse 8; cp. 25: 4f.). *in thy gracious kindness, show me:* the Hebrew reads 'thy spirit is good, lead me', or 'let thy good spirit lead me'. God's spirit is his guiding, life-giving presence (cp. Neh. 9: 20 and see on Ps. 51: 11).

11. *Keep me safe:* literally 'Give me life', and therefore a parallel expression to 'let thy good spirit lead me'. It is precisely for God's life-giving presence that the psalmist thirsts (verses 6f.).

12. *In thy love for me . . .:* this might appear a most selfish prayer, but there is no *for me* in the Hebrew and God's love is the expression of his faithfulness to fulfil his promise to his whole covenant people (see on verse 8 and more fully on 51: 1). Hence it is only as a member of the community of God, as one who has chosen to walk his 'way', that the psalmist can personally make this appeal to his love. The vindication of his servant will therefore help to demonstrate God's active will to uphold his covenant, but in a world where wickedness seems to triumph it must inevitably entail the silencing of oppression. ✶

HAPPY THE PEOPLE WHO HAVE
THE LORD FOR THEIR GOD

144

Blessed is the LORD, my rock,   1
    who trains my hands for war,
    my fingers for battle;
my help that never fails, my fortress,   2
    my strong tower and my refuge,
    my shield in which I trust,
    he who puts nations[a] under my feet.

O LORD, what is man that thou carest for him?   3
What is mankind? Why give a thought to them?
Man is no more than a puff of wind,   4
    his days a passing shadow.
If thou, LORD, but tilt the heavens, down they come;   5
    touch the mountains, and they smoke.
Shoot forth thy lightning flashes, far and wide,   6
    and send thy arrows whistling.
Stretch out thy hands from on high to rescue me   7
    and snatch me from great waters.[b]

I will sing a new song to thee, O God,   9
psalms to the music of a ten-stringed lute.
O God who gavest victory to kings   10
    and deliverance to thy servant David,
rescue me from the cruel sword;
snatch me from the power of foreign foes,   11
    whose every word is false
    and all their oaths are perjury.

[a] *So some MSS.; others* my people.
[b] *Prob. rdg.; Heb. adds* from the power of foreign foes, (8) whose every
word is false and all their oaths are perjury (*cp. verse 11*).

12 Happy^a are we whose sons in their early prime
     stand like tall towers,
   our daughters like sculptured pillars
     at the corners of a palace.
13 Our barns are full and furnish plentiful provision;
   our sheep bear lambs in thousands upon thousands;
14 the oxen in our fields are fat and sleek;
     there is no miscarriage or untimely birth,
     no cries of distress in our public places.
15 Happy are the people in such a case as ours;
   happy the people who have the LORD for their God.

☀ It is very difficult to find an overall plan in this psalm. It opens with thanksgiving to God for his part in the psalmist's victories (verses 1f.) and is followed by a section (verses 3–8) which initially contrasts man's nothingness with God's overwhelming power, before shading into a prayer for deliverance. Verse 9 declares the psalmist's intention to sing praises to God, while verses 10f. repeat the prayer for deliverance. The psalm concludes with either a prayer for material blessing, or a statement that God's people already enjoy such blessing (see the commentary).

   Commentators have pointed out that the psalm seems to be dependent on other psalms (e.g. with verse 3 cp. 8: 4; with verse 5 cp. 18: 9 which is closer to verse 5 than N.E.B. would suggest). We may accept that this is so, but we are not thereby excused from seeking an overall sense for the psalm. As an attempt to give an overall sense, we may say that the psalm asserts that whether in war (verses 1f.) or peace (verses 12–14), true happiness comes only from a proper recognition of man's frailty (verses 3f.), God's might (verses 5–7), and the grateful receiving of all God's gifts (verses 9–10*b*). Such confidence can be the basis for prayer for deliverance (verses

[a] *Prob. rdg.; Heb.* Who.

8, 10c, 11). The reference to David in verse 10 may indicate that the original speaker was the king, or a leader of the people, if the psalm was composed after the exile.

1. *who trains my hands for war:* the idea that God actually instructed the psalmist in the art of warfare is distasteful to modern readers; but it was an easy step from the belief that God assisted the Israelties in battle to the belief that he encouraged their warlike activity. Perhaps we can say that the survival of the Israelite people with the help of war was the necessary raw material, out of which sprang the greater vision of God's universal rule in which implements of war would be needed for peaceful purposes only (Isa. 2: 4).

2. *he who puts nations under my feet:* the alternative reading 'my people' instead of *nations* (N.E.B. footnote) is difficult, because the Hebrew verb has the sense of 'beating down'. Some interpreters prefer 'his feet' for *my feet*.

3–7. The connection between verses 3f. and 5–7 in the Hebrew is not clear, especially as verses 5–7 are characterized by imperatives, literally, 'O Lord, bow thy heavens and come down, touch the mountains . . .' The N.E.B. paraphrases verses 5–7, thus bringing out a contrast between the frailty of man (verses 3f.) and the might of God (verses 5–7).

7. *Stretch out:* having alluded to Ps. 18: 9 and 14 in verses 5f., the psalmist now alludes to verse 16, from which it seems clear that *great waters* are a figure for the psalmist's enemies. A comparison with Ps. 18: 17 suggests that the N.E.B. is wrong to relegate verses 7c–8 to the footnotes, although the occurrence of substantially the same phrase in verse 11 is to be noted. Verses 7f. and 11 could be refrains.

10. *deliverance to thy servant . . .:* Hebrew 'who delivered his servant David from the cruel sword, rescue me . . .' The N.E.B. gives better parallelism.

11. Possibly a refrain, as at verses 7f.

12. *Happy are we:* the connection of these verses with what precedes has long been a problem, and an ancient solution is

to make verses 12–14 refer not to Israel but to her enemies, who are said, however, to be without blessing, for they do not have 'the LORD for their God' (verse 15). Other possibilities are to render verse 12 as a prayer: 'so that our sons may stand . . .', or as looking forward to verse 15: 'when our sons . . . Happy are the people . . .' Although it is difficult to be certain, the present commentary prefers to take verses 12–14 as a prayer for blessing expressed in extravagant language, followed by the exclamation of verse 15, 'Happy are the people . . .' *sculptured pillars:* the reference may include either good looks, or regal stature, or both.

15. *Happy are the people:* for *Happy* see Pss. 1: 1 and 119: 1. To *have the LORD for their God* is not simply to have access to a convenient supply of material benefit. The people of God must be true to their Lord, and in consequence experience the hostility of enemies who prefer the ways of unrighteousness (verse 11). The reward for that loyalty will then be the material benefits described in verses 13f. ✳

I WILL BLESS THY NAME FOR EVER AND EVER

145

1 I will extol thee, O God my king,
   and bless thy name for ever and ever.
2 Every day will I bless thee
   and praise thy name for ever and ever.
3 Great is the LORD and worthy of all praise;
   his greatness is unfathomable.
4 One generation shall commend thy works to another
   and set forth thy mighty deeds.
5 My theme shall be thy marvellous works,
   the glorious splendour of thy majesty.
6 Men shall declare thy mighty acts with awe

and tell[a] of thy great deeds.

They shall recite the story of thy abounding goodness 7
   and sing of thy righteousness with joy.

The LORD is gracious and compassionate, 8
   forbearing, and constant in his love.
The LORD is good to all men, 9
and his tender care rests upon all his creatures.

All thy creatures praise thee, LORD, 10
   and thy servants bless thee.
They talk of the glory of thy kingdom 11
   and tell of thy might,
they proclaim to their fellows how mighty are thy[b] deeds, 12
   how glorious the majesty of thy[b] kingdom.
Thy kingdom is an everlasting kingdom, 13
and thy dominion stands for all generations.

In all his promises the LORD keeps faith, 14
   he is unchanging in all his works;[c]
the LORD holds up those who stumble
   and straightens backs which are bent.
The eyes of all are lifted to thee in hope, 15
and thou givest them their food when it is due;

with open and bountiful hand 16
thou givest what they desire[d] to every living creature.
The LORD is righteous in all his ways, 17
   unchanging in all that he does;
very near is the LORD to those who call to him, 18
   who call to him in singleness of heart.

[a] and tell: *prob. rdg., cp. Sept.; Heb.* I will tell.   [b] *So Sept.; Heb.* his.
[c] In all his promises . . . works: *so Sept.; Heb. om.*
[d] they desire: *or* thou wilt.

19 He fulfils their desire if only they fear him;
    he hears their cry and saves them.
20 The LORD watches over all who love him
    but sends the wicked to their doom.
21 My tongue shall speak out the praises of the LORD,
    and all creatures shall bless his holy name
    for ever and ever.

* Probably no psalm in the whole Psalter is less in need of commentary than Ps. 145. The fact that this is an acrostic psalm in which each verse begins with a new letter of the Hebrew alphabet (see p. 10) means that it consists in the main of short, self-contained statements. These centre on the universal rule of God, and result in an incomparable hymn of praise to God as king, which has occupied a prominent place in both Jewish and Christian worship. It is a fitting beginning to the final section of praise (Pss. 145–150) with which the Psalter concludes. In the psalms scroll from Qumran, each verse is followed by the refrain 'blessed be the LORD, and blessed be his name, for ever and ever'.

1. *for ever and ever:* it is unlikely that the psalmist meant that he would praise God for all eternity; such a view of eternity was probably not yet developed in Israel. But if the psalmist speaks for the whole people of God, then praise to God will be offered for generation after generation by that people.

3. *his greatness is unfathomable:* no human mind can enquire into God's greatness, so as to know its full extent.

6. *thy mighty acts with awe:* the N.E.B. obscures the fact that in the Hebrew *awe* relates to the *mighty acts*, not their declaration. 'Thy awesome mighty acts' could be a possible rendering.

9. *to all men:* God's care for his world extends to all creatures, including all mankind. This does not mean, however, that he does not execute justice against all wickedness (see verse 20). Such moral action is also part of God's wise government.

10. *thy servants*: the Hebrew implies that these servants are those whose relationship with God depends on his covenant with Israel. These servants are thus the best placed of all mankind to proclaim God's kingship to the world.

14. *In all his promises*: this verse, beginning with the Hebrew letter *nun* has now been found in the psalm scroll from Qumran (cp. also the N.E.B. footnote).

18. *in singleness of heart*: 'in truth'. The expression probably includes sincerity, and steadfastness of purpose.

19. *if only they fear him*: *if only* is an interpretation on the part of the N.E.B. It may also be that 'those who fear God' are those whom God has brought into his covenant.

20. *watches over*: actively watches and protects. *to their doom*: the punishment of the wicked is not contrary to, but an expression of, God's gracious government (see on verse 9). ✶

HAPPY IS THE MAN WHOSE HELPER
IS THE GOD OF JACOB

146

O praise the LORD.   1

Praise the LORD, my soul.
As long as I live I will praise the LORD;   2
   I will sing psalms to my God all my life long.
Put no faith in princes,   3
   in any man, who has no power to save.
   He breathes his last breath,   4
   he returns to the dust;
and in that same hour all his thinking ends.

Happy the man whose helper is the God of Jacob,   5
   whose hopes are in the LORD his God,
maker of heaven and earth,   6
   the sea, and all that is in them;

who serves wrongdoers as he has sworn
7　　　and deals out justice to the oppressed.
The LORD feeds the hungry
　　　and sets the prisoner free.
8　The LORD restores sight to the blind
　　　and straightens backs which are bent;
the LORD loves the righteous
9　　　and watches over the stranger;
the LORD gives heart to the orphan and widow
but turns the course of the wicked to their ruin.
10　The LORD shall reign for ever,
　　　thy God, O Zion, for all generations.

O praise the LORD.

* Pss. 146–150 begin and end with the phrase 'O praise the LORD' and are described as 'Hallelujah' psalms (after the Hebrew for 'O praise the LORD'; see on Ps. 106: 1). Ps. 146 contrasts the gracious power of God, which manifests itself in action on behalf of the oppressed and in judgement against the wicked (verses 5–10), with the powerlessness of man to establish a true order (verses 3f.). The fact of God's gracious power is the ground for the psalmist's declaration that he will praise God as long as he lives (verses 1f.). The psalm contains echoes of Ps. 145 (cp. Ps. 145: 14 with 146: 8), and it is usually thought, on linguistic grounds, to be a late psalm.

3. *Put no faith in princes: princes* are noble and powerful people, who probably control the affairs of state. The psalmist does not condemn nobility as such, nor human government; but he recognizes that princes share all the limitations of mortal men, and their power must not become the object of unwavering trust. *no power to save:* in the light of verses 6–10 *save* is best understood as establishing the sort of order in which there is no injustice.

4. *all his thinking ends:* even if a ruler has good plans and intentions, those die with him, and he may be replaced by others with different aims. This continual flux contrasts with the permanence of God's will for mankind.

5. *the God of Jacob:* cp. Ps. 46: 7, 11, where the title *God of Jacob* is especially associated with help and protection.

6–10. The psalmist was presumably sufficient of a realist to know that what is described in these verses represents God's ideal will, and that this ideal will was only partially manifested in a world where mortal man had so much real power. The psalmist could have pointed to past historical periods, and to individual examples, as instances where God's ideal will was especially to be seen. But in verse 10, *The LORD shall reign*, there is an element of looking forward to the full realization in the world of God's ideal will. The psalmist knows something of the tension between the 'already' and the 'not yet'; but the 'already' is still sufficient to provoke unending praise from the psalmist (verses 1f.), in a situation where the power of the 'princes' is perhaps all too evident. ✳

HIS PLEASURE IS IN THOSE WHO FEAR HIM

147

O praise the LORD.   1

How good it is to sing psalms to our God!
    How pleasant[a] to praise him!
The LORD is rebuilding Jerusalem;   2
    he gathers in the scattered sons of Israel.
It is he who heals the broken in spirit   3
    and binds up their wounds,
he who numbers the stars one by one   4
    and names them one and all.

[a] *So Sept.; Heb. adds* right.

5 Mighty is our Lord and great his power,
    and his wisdom beyond all telling.

6 The LORD gives new heart to the humble
    and brings evildoers down to the dust.

7 Sing to the LORD a song of thanksgiving,
    sing psalms to the harp in honour of our God.

8 He veils the sky in clouds
    and prepares rain for the earth;
    he clothes the hills with grass
    and green plants for the use of man.[a]

9 He gives the cattle their food
    and the young ravens all that they gather.

10 The LORD sets no store by the strength of a horse
    and takes no pleasure in a runner's legs;

11 his pleasure is in those who fear him,
    who wait for his true love.

12 Sing to the LORD, Jerusalem;
    O Zion, praise your God,

13 for he has put new bars in your gates;
    he has blessed your children within them.

14 He has brought peace to your realm
    and given you fine wheat in plenty.

15 He sends his command to the ends of the earth,
    and his word runs swiftly.

16 He showers down snow, white as wool,
    and sprinkles hoar-frost thick as ashes;

17 crystals of ice he scatters like bread-crumbs;
    he sends the cold, and the water stands frozen,

18 he utters his word, and the ice is melted;
    he blows with his wind and the waters flow.

[a] and green . . . man: *so Sept.; Heb. om.*

To Jacob he makes his word known,   19
   his statutes and decrees to Israel;
he has not done this for any other nation,   20
   nor taught them his decrees.

O praise the LORD.

✻ The N.E.B. prints this psalm with a break at verse 11. This corresponds to the fact that in the Greek numbering (see pp. 2f.), verses 1–11 form Ps. 146, and verses 12–20 form Ps. 147. However, the psalm is probably to be divided into three sections, verses 1–6, 7–11 and 12–20. Each section begins with a command to worship God (in verse 1 it is 'O praise the LORD', which is more closely integrated with the rest of the verse than the N.E.B. suggests), followed by an enumeration of God's mighty deeds in nature, and towards the humble and those who fear him. On the basis of verses 2 and 13, it has been suggested that the psalm was composed at the time of Nehemiah (445 B.C.) when the walls of Jerusalem were being rebuilt and the city repopulated (Neh. 4, 7). Although this is possible, it is not certain; and in the context of the psalm, the references to Jerusalem and Israel indicate that although God's power is generally to be discerned in the natural order, it is only on the basis of grace which is directed towards his people, that Israel can praise a God who is to be served and known as a person.

1. *O praise the LORD:* see on Ps. 106: 1. Although this phrase precedes and follows each of Pss. 146–150, the phrase here is closely linked with the rest of verse 1, and is similar to 'Sing to the LORD' in verses 7 and 12. *How pleasant:* although the N.E.B. has omitted a word with the Septuagint (see footnote), it is probably to be retained on poetic and textual grounds, producing the rendering 'How pleasant to make fitting praise!'

2. *rebuilding:* or 'is building', in the sense of continually caring for Jerusalem and its development. *scattered sons:*

there may be a specific reference to Israelites who were dismayed by the ill-fortunes of the people prior to the arrival of Nehemiah; but more probably this is a general expression for divine help.

4. *numbers the stars:* possibly, the psalmist is denying that the stars and planets shape the destinies of men and nations.

6. *gives new heart:* cp. Ps. 146: 9, where the thought of this verse is expressed more fully.

7. *Sing to the LORD:* this begins the second section.

8. *green plants:* the fourth line of this verse is probably lost from the Hebrew, and is restored from the Septuagint.

9. *young ravens:* cp. Job 38: 41. It may have been a popular, but unfounded, belief that young ravens were abandoned by their parents, and thus depended entirely upon God for their survival.

10f. *sets no store:* in contrast to the animals, who rely upon God, there are men who rely on their own strength; but this blinds them to the presence and power of God, whose *pleasure is in those who fear him.*

12. *Sing to the LORD:* the beginning of the third section; cp. verse 7.

13. *he has put new bars:* wooden bars, in order to secure the gates against enemies.

15. *He sends his command:* this verse probably sums up what follows in verses 15–20, where God's word directs and sustains the course of nature (verse 18), and makes known the divine will to Israel (verse 19). In this, two ideas are brought together. First, that God created the world by speaking a word of command (cp. Gen. 1 and the repeated formula 'God said, "Let there be . . ."' See also Ps. 33: 6, 9, 'The LORD's word made the heavens . . . For he spoke, and it was'); second, that in giving the ten 'words' or commandments to his people (Deut. 4: 13), he made known his 'decrees and statutes'. In later Judaism, 'word' can be a way of referring to God himself, and in the New Testament the belief is expressed that the word has become man (John 1: 14). This psalm con-

tains one of the most striking expressions in the Old Testament of God's activity in the natural and moral world, in terms of his 'word'.

17. *the water stands frozen:* this translation involves a slight rearrangement of the Hebrew consonants, which in their traditional order mean 'who can withstand his cold?'

20. *he has not done this:* Israel alone has been chosen for a special relationship with God, but this confers responsibility (Amos 3: 1f.). Although God has not taught the nations his decrees he has been concerned about them (Amos 9: 7; Deut. 32: 8) and will hold them responsible for injustice (Amos 1–2). The nations are part of God's creation, and as such, receive the care for his creation which this psalm expresses. ✷

LET ALL PRAISE THE NAME OF THE LORD

148

O praise the LORD. 1

Praise the LORD out of heaven;
 praise him in the heights.
Praise him, all his angels; 2
 praise him, all his host.
Praise him, sun and moon; 3
 praise him, all you shining stars;
praise him, heaven of heavens, 4
 and you waters above the heavens.
Let them all praise the name of the LORD, 5
for he spoke the word and they were created;
he established them for ever and ever 6
by an ordinance which shall never pass away.

Praise the LORD from the earth, 7
 you water-spouts and ocean depths;

8   fire and hail, snow and ice,
           gales of wind obeying his voice;
9   all mountains and hills;
           all fruit-trees and all cedars;
10   wild beasts and cattle,
           creeping things and winged birds;
11   kings and all earthly rulers,
           princes and judges over the whole earth;
12   young men and maidens,
           old men and young together.
13   Let all praise the name of the LORD,
           for his name is high above all others,
           and his majesty above earth and heaven;
14   he has exalted his people in the pride of power[a]
           and crowned with praise his loyal servants,
           all Israel, the people nearest him.

           O praise the LORD.

✳ This psalm is in two parts, verses 1–6 and 7–14. In the first part, the created things belonging to the heavens are called upon to praise God, and in verses 7–14, the command for praise is addressed to the realm of the earth. The list of created things mentioned in the psalm has been compared with Job 38 in the Hebrew Bible, and with Ecclus. 43 and the Song of the Three in the Apocrypha, and with certain Egyptian texts. However, Ps. 148 probably stands closer to Gen. 1: 1 – 2: 4a than any of these other texts. Verses 1–6 correspond to Gen. 1: 1–19, the creation of the heavenly bodies, while verses 7–14 correspond to Gen. 1: 20 – 2: 4a. Although Ps. 148 contains material not found in Gen. 1, there are similarities of language, as well as ideas, and the psalm reflects the 'word theology' of Gen. 1 (see on Ps. 147: 15). It would not

[a] exalted . . . power: *lit.* raised up a horn for his people.

be unfair to describe the psalm as a version of Gen. 1 suitable for use as a hymn. An open question is whether verse 14*b–c* should be translated 'A hymn of praise for all his loyal servants, for all Israel, the people nearest to him', and should be regarded either as a title for Ps. 148 placed at the end, or as the title for Ps. 149. The psalm is usually held to have been composed after the exile.

1. *O praise the LORD:* see on Ps. 106: 1, and the introduction to Ps. 146 (p. 178). *out of heaven:* the things pertaining to the heavenly part of the creation; contrast verse 7, 'from the earth'.

2. *angels . . . host:* God's heavenly court, whose members obey his commands, and put them into effect in the world.

4. *heaven of heavens:* cp. 1 Kings 8: 27 (Authorized Version or Revised Version). Possibly, the psalmist believed that there were several heavens, and is saying 'highest heaven'. *waters above the heavens:* cp. Gen. 1: 6f.

5. *he spoke the word:* or, 'it was he (and no other) who spoke the word' (literally 'it was he who commanded'). The idea of creation by the divine word or command must be seen in the light of the Old Testament conception of God, who commands his people, and speaks his word of promise and judgement (and see on Ps. 147: 15).

6. *which shall never pass away:* the constituent parts of the created heavens cannot act arbitrarily, but only according to a fixed and regular pattern.

7. *water-spouts:* see Gen. 1: 21, where the N.E.B. has 'sea-monsters' for the same Hebrew word, thus obscuring the parallel between Gen. 1 and this psalm. The reference in this verse may also be to all the great creatures that live in the sea.

8. *fire:* i.e. lightning. *ice:* Hebrew probably, 'thick smoke'. The N.E.B. follows the Septuagint and Vulgate here.

9f. Cp. Gen. 1: 21, 24f.

11f. The detail of the various distinctions of rank and sex implies that the distinctions are ordained by God, and part of his created order. Human society is intended to be no less ordered than the natural world, and the perspective is not that of Israel alone, but man, as the final act of creation (Gen. 1: 26).

13. *Let all praise:* all those things mentioned from verse 7 onwards. If distinctions of rank are ordained by God, it is so that human society may be justly ordered, and thus able to render thanks to the creator. *his majesty above earth and heaven:* although God's glory may be discerned in and through the natural order, in essence and being he transcends the creation.

14. If this verse is not part of a title (see above; the N.E.B. paraphrases the Hebrew), the psalm goes beyond Gen. 1 and speaks of God's choosing of Israel. However, the purpose of God's choosing of Israel is to bring all mankind to the acknowledgement of God's rule, so that all mankind utters the praise expressed in this psalm. ✳

LET HIS FAITHFUL SERVANTS EXULT IN TRIUMPH

149

1   O praise the LORD.

    Sing to the LORD a new song,
       sing his praise in the assembly of the faithful;
2   let Israel rejoice in his maker
       and the sons of Zion exult in their king.
3   Let them praise his name in the dance,
       and sing him psalms with tambourine and harp.
4   For the LORD accepts the service of his people;
       he crowns his humble folk with victory.
5   Let his faithful servants exult in triumph;
       let them shout for joy as they kneel before him.
6   Let the high praises of God be on their lips
       and a two-edged sword in their hand,

> to wreak vengeance on the nations   7
>   and to chastise the heathen;
> to load their kings with chains   8
>   and put their nobles in irons;
> to execute the judgement decreed against them–   9
> this is the glory of all his faithful servants.

> O praise the LORD.

* The modern reader of the psalm will usually find verses 1–5 an acceptable and vigorous expression of praise to God, but is likely to be repelled by the warlike tone of verses 6–9. There have been various attempts to account for this warlike tone. The psalm has been dated to the time of Nehemiah's rebuilding of the walls of Jerusalem (445 B.C.; see Neh. 4) or to the Maccabaean revolt (167 B.C.); or the psalm has been traced to a cultic drama in which the worshippers symbolically defeated the powers of evil. Whatever view we take, we cannot avoid the fact that in parts of the Old Testament, the task of Israel was conceived as a holy war, the object of which was to destroy the nations that did not acknowledge God (cp. Joshua). Something of that same view is to be found here. The enemies of Israel are also the enemies of God, and they possibly include not only physical enemies, but the hostile realms of death and darkness (and cp. Ps. 139: 19–22). These closing verses proclaim that God's rule can ultimately allow no rival rule in the world; and it by no means encourages an idle indifference to all that is contrary to God's rule.

1 *O praise the LORD:* see on Ps. 106: 1 and the introduction to Ps. 146 (p. 178). *a new song:* a song occasioned by God's grace, and the revelation of his will. *sing his praise . . . the faithful:* the Hebrew closely resembles Ps. 148: 14*b*, and the present psalm may be a continuation of Ps. 148.

2. *his maker:* as a people, Israel has been brought into being, and sustained, by God.

4. *accepts the service of his people: service* is an interpretation; perhaps the Hebrew 'takes pleasure in his people' is merely another way of stating God's choice of Israel.

5. *as they kneel before him:* the traditional rendering, 'on their beds', has sometimes been used to justify failure to attend early-morning services! If 'on their beds' is correct, then praise day and night is meant. The N.E.B. rendering fits well with the rest of the psalm.

6. *two-edged sword:* the phrase denotes either a double-bladed axe, or a sharp, devouring sword.

8. *load their kings with chains:* having defeated them.

9. *the judgement decreed:* the sentence passed by God (cp. Amos 1–2). *this is the glory: glory* here has the sense of an honour or privilege that is conferred upon a person. It is to be hoped that God's *faithful servants* who enjoy the privilege of carrying out the *judgement decreed* would do so with great humility. Perhaps the phrase 'humble folk' in verse 4 indicates that this might be so. ✻

PRAISE THE LORD

150

1   O praise the LORD.

O praise God in his holy place,
praise him in the vault of heaven, the vault of his
        power;
2   praise him for his mighty works,
        praise him for his immeasurable greatness.
3   Praise him with fanfares on the trumpet,
        praise him upon lute and harp;
4   praise him with tambourines and dancing,
        praise him with flute and strings;
5   praise him with the clash of cymbals,
        praise him with triumphant cymbals;

6 let everything that has breath praise the LORD!

O praise the LORD.

✳ Whether or not this psalm was written with the express intention of bringing the Psalter to a conclusion it does so magnificently, and in words that can still thrill a worshipping congregation. Speculation about its date and form can add nothing to the power of its content. See *Old Testament Illustrations*, pp. 130f. for information about some of the musical instruments mentioned in the psalm.

1. *O praise the LORD:* see on Ps. 106: 1 and the introduction to Ps. 146 (p. 178). *his holy place:* possibly, both his dwelling beyond the heavens, and the temple in Jerusalem, the immediate location of the music and dancing of verses 3–5. *the vault of heaven, the vault of his power:* it is a pity that the phrase *the vault of his power*, which tries to spell out what the preceding words mean, spoils the poetry. The Hebrew refers to the vault (Gen. 1: 6) which supported the waters above it, and the phrase probably means 'the vault which is a sign of his power'.

2. *mighty works:* in creating, choosing and redeeming.

4. *strings:* these will be plucked instruments.

6. *everything that has breath:* the whole creation, but crowned by man who has the unique knowledge and skills needed to offer worship to the creator. ✳

A NOTE ON FURTHER READING

For background and comparative material see J. B. Pritchard, *Ancient Near Eastern Texts* (3rd ed., Princeton University Press, 1969).

For introductory books on the psalms see C. F. Barth, *Introduction to the Psalms* (Blackwell, 1966); H. Ringgren, *The Faith of the Psalmists* (S.C.M. Press, 1963); C. Westermann, *The Praise of God in the Psalms* (John Knox Press, Richmond, Virginia, 1965).

For a more comprehensive and detailed commentary see A. A. Anderson, *Psalms*, New Century Bible (Oliphants, 1972).

For a more conservative approach see D. Kidner, *Psalms*, Tyndale Old Testament Commentaries (Inter-Varsity Press, 1973–5). For an older, but extremely valuable, commentary see A. F. Kirkpatrick, *The Book of Psalms*, The Cambridge Bible for Schools and Colleges (Cambridge University Press, 1891–1901).

INDEX

Aaron 39, 44, 68, 78, 85
Abel 140
Abimelech 37
Abiram 161
Abraham 33, 36f.
Absalom 140
abyss, *see* deep
acrostic psalms 10, 69, 89, 176
angel(s) 26, 29, 185
animal symbolism 121
antiphonal psalms 115
Arabia 114
Ark of the Covenant 6, 34, 36, 137f.
Asaph 4f.

Babylon 40, 48, 51, 150f.
Belial 17

Cain 140
Caleb 47
Christian interpretation 15, 22, 53, 59, 66, 83, 88, 126, 132
coronation 1, 16, 66f.
covenant (covenant faith, Sinai covenant) 36, 41, 48, 60, 70, 83, 144, 170, 177; with David 1, 8, 137
covenant people 33, 36, 40, 83, 170, 186, 188
curses 59–63, 129–31, 150f.
Cyrus 151

Dathan 161
David 2–7, 34, 66f., 117f., 137f., 140, 167, 173
David, author of psalms 2–4, 7
David, house of 1, 16, 117f., 137–9
Day of Atonement 43
death 25, 52, 79, 81f., 166, 169; *see also* Sheol
deep 29, 32, 53, 121, 132, 173
demonic and other terrifying imagery 17, 169, 187

doubt 2, 132
doxologies 3, 6, 48
drama (ritual) 187

Edom 58, 151
Egypt 27, 36–40, 76
Elijah 108
Elohistic Psalter 4f.
enemies *see* evildoers
Ephraim 58
Ephrathah 138
Esau 140
eschatological pictures 179
evildoers 6f., 16, 54, 59, 62f., 67, 72, 99, 105–7, 110, 114, 122, 129–31, 150, 156, 159–64, 166, 168f., 173f., 187
exile, Babylonian 17f., 21f., 24f., 34, 40, 47–51, 70, 75, 78, 83, 87–9, 114, 118f., 124, 130, 136, 139, 148, 150f., 153, 163, 173, 185
exodus 37–43, 50, 70, 75, 130, 145, 147f.

faith 2, 82, 115, 122
festivals 16, 43, 74, 83, 118, 124, 128, 137, 140
Flood, *see* deep
folly 52, 62
forgiveness 26, 132f.
form criticism 7f.

Gilead 58
Glory 21, 44, 57, 74, 78, 186, 188
God
  as creator 22, 26–33, 44, 70, 74–6, 103, 116, 121, 144, 147–9, 158, 182–4, 186, 189
  as judge 26f., 33, 48, 60, 64, 114, 122f., 129f., 151, 159, 176, 178, 185, 188
  as warrior 58, 173
  eternity of 22